©1986 by Camden House Publishing Inc.
First printing January 1985; second printing September 1985.

Canadian Cataloguing in Publication Data
The Harrowsmith Tomato Handbook
ISBN 0-920656-36-6
1. Tomatoes   I. Bennett, Jennifer   II. Harrowsmith
SB349.H37 1985   635′.642   C85-098413-0

Printed in Canada by
RBW Graphics, Owen Sound, Ontario, for

Camden House Publishing Inc.
The Creamery
Charlotte, Vermont 05445

Front Cover: Photograph by Yuri Dojc/The Stock Market

Back Cover: Ontario Ministry of Agriculture and Food

The Harrowsmith

TOMATO
HANDBOOK

Edited by Jennifer Bennett

CAMDEN HOUSE

Contents

The Chilly Immigrant

Tomato Tactics for the Northern Gardener

That it is by nature not well suited to their climate is little discouragement to northern gardeners determined to grow the tomato, most popular of all garden crops. In recent years, it has grown bigger, redder, more disease-resistant and farther north in more gardens than ever before, even as the consumption of less favored vegetables, such as its cousin the potato, has plummeted. Helped by the work of agricultural researchers and plant breeders, the northern gardener is extending both tomato season and tomato range with a bag of horticultural tricks that includes plastic, the proper plants and prayer.

The object of all this devotion is *Lycopersicon esculentum*, a plant native to equatorial South America, where temperatures seldom dip below 50 de-

Despite its tropical origins, the tomato can be coaxed to produce a delicious harvest even in cool gardens.

7

grees F and the tiny-fruited wild tomatoes are able to survive year-round on the tropical mountain slopes. When the New World plant was brought to the Old by 16th-century explorers, however, the European climate was not alone in granting it a cool reception. The fruits the explorers introduced were large and succulent in appearance, evidence of generations of tomato selection in South and Central America; yet, related as it was to familiar members of the botanical family Solanaceae such as mandrake and deadly nightshade, the plant was dubbed *mala insana*, the unwholesome fruit, by Europeans, and was considered reliable only as a decorative shrub, the love apple. It was Italian cuisine that first embraced the newcomer, and it still dominates in pizza, spaghetti and minestrone.

In North America, suspicion of the tomato lingered until Robert Gibbon Johnson ate a ripe one on the steps of the courthouse of Salem, New Jersey, in 1820, in full and foolhardy view of all—and survived. Soon the tomato's popularity began to skyrocket, and the versatile vegetable continued to gain devotees even in the 20th century. Per capita tomato consumption in the United States has trebled since 1920.

Furthermore, according to the National Garden Bureau of the United States, tomatoes are the most valuable of garden vegetables when both space efficiency and market value are taken into consideration. A single plant can produce 20 pounds of fruit which, at a market value of 80 cents a pound, could result in a $16.00 harvest of flavor and nutrients from only a few square feet of garden space.

FRUIT AND VEGETABLE

Botanically speaking, tomatoes are the fruit of a vine, just as are cucumbers, squashes, beans and peas. But in the common language of the people, whether sellers or consumers of provisions, all these are vegetables which are grown in kitchen gardens and which, whether eaten cooked or raw, are, like potatoes, carrots, parsnips, turnips, beets, cauliflower, cabbage, celery and lettuce, usually served at dinner in, with or after the soup, fish or meats which constitute the principal part of the repast and not, like fruits generally, as dessert.

—Associate Justice Horace Gray of the United States Supreme Court in deciding whether tomatoes should be taxed as fruits or vegetables, 1883

Fortunately, the tomato is not only popular but gratifyingly wholesome too. A glass of tomato juice contains about four times as much vitamin A and roughly half as much vitamin C as the same amount of orange juice. Fresh tomatoes carry a respectable amount of vitamins A and C as well as calcium and potassium. To some extent, this vitamin content is related to ripeness. Studies have shown that as a tomato ripens, its hardness, starch content and acidity decrease, while its pigment, vitamin C and soluble sugars rise, good incentive to let it linger in the sun until fully ripe—if possible.

But neither climate nor weather is always coop-

erative. Plant breeders have shaved weeks from the maturation requirements of some tomatoes, allowing gardeners in cool areas to grow not only small and cherry tomatoes but also some of the big, flattened beefsteaks and the pear- or plum-shaped Ital-

NEAPOLITAN LOVE APPLES

"When ripe, the fruit, which has an acid flavor, is put into soups and sauces, and the juice is preserved for winter use, like catsup; it is also used in confectionary, as a preserve and, when green, as a pickle. Though a good deal used in England in soups and as a principal ingredient in a well-known sauce for mutton, yet our estimation and uses of the fruit are nothing to those of the French and Italians, and especially the latter. Near Rome and Naples, whole fields are covered with it; and scarcely a dinner is served up in which it does not, in some way or other, form a part."

— *John Loudon, in Thomas G. Fessenden's*
New American Gardener, *1843*

FROST DATE DATA

The following average last spring and first fall frost dates are from *The Weather Almanac* (4th edition) — "featuring the newly released climatic normals for 1951-1980" — edited by James A. Ruffner and Frank E. Blair.

	Last Spring Frost	*First Fall Frost*		*Last Spring Frost*	*First Fall Frost*
ALASKA			IDAHO		
Anchorage	May 18	September 13	Boise	April 29	October 16
Nome	June 12	August 24	Pocatello	May 8	September 30
CALIFORNIA			ILLINOIS		
Bakersfield	February 14	November 28	Chicago	April 19	October 28
Sacramento	January 24	December 11	Springfield	April 8	October 30
COLORADO			INDIANA		
Denver	May 2	October 14	Fort Wayne	April 24	October 20
Pueblo	April 28	October 12	Indianapolis	April 17	October 27
CONNECTICUT			IOWA		
Hartford	April 22	October 19	Des Moines	April 20	October 19
New Haven	April 15	October 27	Dubuque	April 19	October 19
DIST. OF COLUMBIA	April 10	October 28	KANSAS		
			Dodge City	April 22	October 24
			Topeka	April 9	October 26

	Last Spring Frost	First Fall Frost		Last Spring Frost	First Fall Frost
KENTUCKY			**MISSOURI**		
Lexington	April 13	October 28	Kansas City	April 5	October 31
Louisville	April 1	November 7	St. Louis	April 2	November 8
MAINE			**MONTANA**		
Greenville	May 27	September 20	Billings	May 15	September 24
Portland	April 29	October 15	Superior	June 5	August 30
MARYLAND			**NEBRASKA**		
Annapolis	March 4	November 15	Norfolk	May 4	October 3
Baltimore	March 28	November 17	Omaha	April 14	October 20
MASSACHUSETTS			**NEVADA**		
Boston	April 16	October 25	Elko	June 6	September 3
Nantucket	April 12	November 16	Las Vegas	May 13	November 13
MICHIGAN			**NEW HAMPSHIRE**		
Detroit	April 25	October 23	Concord	May 11	September 30
Sault Ste. Marie	May 18	October 3			
			NEW JERSEY		
MINNESOTA			Cape May	April 4	November 15
Duluth	May 22	September 24	Trenton	April 8	November 5
Minneapolis	April 30	October 13			

	Last Spring Frost	First Fall Frost		Last Spring Frost	First Fall Frost
NEW YORK			**UTAH**		
Albany	April 27	October 13	Blanding	May 18	October 14
Buffalo	April 30	October 25	Salt Lake City	April 12	November 1
NORTH DAKOTA			**VERMONT**		
Bismarck	May 11	September 24	Burlington	May 8	October 3
Fargo	May 13	September 27			
			VIRGINIA		
OHIO			Norfolk	March 18	November 27
Cincinnati	April 15	October 20	Roanoke	April 20	October 24
Cleveland	April 21	November 2			
			WASHINGTON		
OREGON			Seattle	February 23	December 1
Bend	June 17	August 17	Spokane	April 20	October 12
Portland	February 25	December 1			
			WEST VIRGINIA		
PENNSYLVANIA			Charleston	April 18	October 28
Philadelphia	March 30	November 17	Parkersburg	April 16	October 21
Scranton	April 24	October 14			
			WISCONSIN		
RHODE ISLAND			Green Bay	May 6	October 13
Providence	April 13	October 27	Milwaukee	April 20	October 25
SOUTH DAKOTA			**WYOMING**		
Rapid City	May 7	October 4	Cheyenne	May 20	September 27
Sioux Falls	May 5	October 3	Lander	May 15	September 20

ian tomatoes, best for sauces. But frost often cuts the season shorter than the gardener might wish. The tomato is an easy, prolific plant to grow, provided its needs are met, but primary among these needs are plenty of warmth and sunshine, legacy of the South American mountain slopes. A dip to freezing temperatures in either spring or fall (or, for the unlucky, in midsummer) can easily kill it.

The knowledge of one's likely spring and fall frost dates can enable most gardeners to grow tomatoes outdoors, provided they start the plants under cover and are prepared to cover them again whenever the need arises. Row frames, hot caps to cover individual plants, greenhouses, indoor hydroponic units under fluorescent lights and tubs on porches have all been used successfully by the Northerner who will not let a few difficulties of place and time stand in the way of a fresh, home-grown tomato.

The lengths to which some will go may hint of a mild-mannered madness, but only those who have tasted the tropical fruits of a cool, northern summer can really understand that tomatoes are, frankly, worth it.

— JB

ACCORDING TO HORTUS

TOMATO
(*Lycopersicon esculentum* and *L. pimpinellifolium*)
Tender herbs grown as annuals for the much-prized fruits, both out-of-doors and under glass. The husk tomato and strawberry tomato are *Physalis* and the tree tomato, *Cyphomandra betacea*. The tomato is closely allied to the potato, and it is possible to graft one on the other: see POTOMATO.

POTOMATO: A name once applied to the combination potato-tomato plant produced by grafting one on the other. The grafting can be performed either way, but the hope that by this means one can produce good crops of both potatoes and tomatoes on the same plant is fanciful, although both tubers and tomatoes may be produced if the potato is the stock.
— *L.H. Bailey*
Hortus, *1935*

View From the Top

The Master Gardeners Speak

Five master gardeners—Richard Eichenauer and Harue Kanemitsu; Maryanne Ashleigh; Don and Kathy Dill; Walter and Maria Gosse; and Patrick Lima and John Scanlan—told us their secrets for raising bumper crops of tomatoes organically. Taken together, they cover gardening conditions that stretch the length of the north country—and techniques that use those conditions to advantage.

NORTHWEST BONANZA

Richard Eichenauer and Harue Kanemitsu garden in the Pacific Northwest.

Three hundred and twenty-five tomato plants, a whole hillside of them overlooking the Lower Arrow Lake: that was what we grew in our first gar-

In spring, Richard Eichenauer prepares the raised beds that will soon hold his home-grown tomato transplants.

15

den here 20 years ago. With little gardening knowledge to back us up, we associated red tomatoes, rightly enough, with vitamin C and juicy good health. Good health we wanted – the more the better – so rather than discarding all the little seedlings that came up in our first seed flat, we planted them all. In the fall, we did pick a few ripe, red fruits, but by far, the bulk of the tomatoes were still green.

The next year, we reduced our plantation by more than half, to 120 plants, which produced about the same yield of red tomatoes plus a six-gallon vat of pickled green tomatoes, most of which ended up on the compost heap the following spring. The cabin shelves and loft were lined with green tomatoes. A few did ripen indoors, their flavor not always the best, and we had a good supply of mushy ones, just right for a Rossini first night at La Scala in Milano. Unfortunately, we were 8000 miles too far away to contribute to the *beaux-arts*.

But we were learning about gardening. Since those beginning years, we have grown fewer and fewer tomato plants and harvested more and more red, ripe fruit, simply by taking better care of the few plants we grow.

Important to our present success is *Doukhobor*, which is very similar, perhaps the same, as the *Siberia* tomato sold by Siberia Seeds in Montana. This is a very compact tomato of Russian or Siberian origin, with thick foliage and a tolerance to cold that is outstanding. The little plants literally radiate strength and hardiness, yielding red, ripe fruit in August and September, before frosts occur here. We originally received *Doukhobor* seeds from friends in Brilliant, British Columbia, and we have been saving the seeds to give to our friends and neighbors ever since.

We save tomato seeds by scooping them out of the earliest red tomatoes onto a small cotton cloth or paper towel and letting them dry. The seeds stick to the cloth or paper when dry and can be folded up and stored as is, or they can be gently picked or scraped off and put into an envelope or glass jar. The more elaborate method of fermenting the pulp off the seeds is probably better for larger batches, but this simple way works for us.

We start the seeds in mid-March in seed flats on a rack above the stove, covering the flats with thin aluminum (printer's) sheets or a piece of plastic foil to prevent the top layer of soil from drying out. After a few days, we check daily for emerging sprouts and pick out any weeds. We do not sterilize most seed-flat soil.

As soon as the first tomato sprout appears, the seed flat is moved to a rack underneath a skylight in the house or to the greenhouse in front of a heat-retaining stone wall, where there is plenty of light

Elayne Sears in Home Gardening Wisdom/Garden Way

and the temperature is cool, at least at night. We also start some flats of tomatoes directly in the greenhouse, where they take a little longer to emerge but where all danger of spindly or leggy plants is avoided.

Once the plants are two or three inches tall, we transplant them to individual pint- or half-liter-sized containers, such as tin cans, yogurt or milk containers or plastic pots. When they are five to seven inches tall, we transplant those that will remain in the greenhouse into the greenhouse beds, while the ones meant for outdoor growth are transplanted into one-gallon-sized black plastic pots that are kept in the greenhouse until outside temperatures have become warm and stable, usually the end of May or early June. Even then, the plants are not guaranteed success. June 1984 was so cold that the transplants we set out became stunted and never produced as well as they had done in previous years.

When transplanting, we make a point of gathering the entire root ball in one piece, having watered the pot well a day previously and having also watered the hole in the ground where the young plant will go. If the weather is hot and dry, shades around each plant are well worth the bother, but in other weather, we do not use them.

The Pfeiffer Garden Book, a biodynamic guide, states that tomatoes can be fertilized with partly **17** broken-down compost or almost raw, mixed manure, and I have had occasion to resort to this practice in some years when all the mature compost had already been used around earlier vegetables by the time the tomatoes were ready for transplanting. But I no longer use such unfinished organic fertilizers, as I believe that they cause rampant vegetative growth as well as soft fruit that spoils easily. I have overmanured tomatoes and found myself in a jungle of branches and foliage, needing to come back every two or three weeks to prune suckers for hours, carting away more green stuff than I leave on the plants. At that time, we thought that tomatoes would make a prolific green-manure crop. We now turn into the tomato patch only well-behaved bushes that bear solid, firm fruit.

We have never had problems with pests and diseases of tomatoes (a few slugs excepted), perhaps because of luck and our isolated forest location, perhaps because of good organic management. Well-matured compost is important, as is cleaning the garden beds of any leftover vines, stalks and leaves in fall. These can go into the compost bin. Add a bit of soil or manure if possible, layer by layer, and see it steam even during cold fall days, melting the first snow that falls on the bin. The more the gardener can confine the rotting and disintegrating to where they belong, in the compost heap, the less they will

occur the following season in the planting beds.

Although the determinate types of tomatoes are supposed to require no pruning, I have found that I often do prune some of the tomatoes, especially the *Starfires*, but never the *Doukhobors*. As a rule, I let the main stem and the first four suckers grow but remove later suckers, and I prune late in the summer, when I can see what will still make ripe fruit before fall. Then I remove whole side stems with flowers and even little tomatoes on them, but I always leave all the branches that bear only foliage. In fall, we pick the most promising green and yellow tomatoes and place them on windowsills and

18

other available shelves to ripen.

Our determinate, or bush-type, tomatoes are also staked. For several reasons, we feel that we and the plants benefit from their being supported on stakes, often two per plant, which we drive into the ground before planting beside them. First, we tie the main stem and, later, the side branches to the stakes, keeping rain-splashed soil from covering the foliage and fruit. This elevation gives the tomatoes more light and air, preventing mould and spoilage in damp weather.

As the plants fill all the available space around them, the stakes let us know where the centers of the plants are so that we can shuffle our way through the vague passages between them, avoiding stepping on main stems and branches. Also, when the tomatoes are planted in a block of two or three rows, and the stakes are all the same height, about 3½ feet, and nicely lined up with one another, we can pin a horizontal pole across each row of stakes, using these horizontals as supports for tarps to prevent frost damage in early fall. (A local rule is, when the temperature at 10 p.m. drops below 45 degrees F, cover the tomatoes; if the temperature is still above 45, it will probably not freeze that night.) This sounds like a lot of bother, but often, we have only a few nights of frost in late August or early September and then have balmy weather for another month or so. We would have lost all that growing and ripening time had we not covered the plants. After all, the main work is done, and the tomatoes are just about ripe, so why withhold a little care and trouble on chilly evenings? I have always enjoyed going outdoors by myself or with a friend or our kids to put the tomatoes, squashes and peppers to bed. The stars are often bright, and sometimes, we are rewarded with the spectacle of the northern lights. It is during those moments that the freshness of this universe, the great outdoors right in front of my home – in fact, this great outdoors that is my home – gives me unspeakable satisfaction and inspiration. It's no bother at all. It's what I live for.

NORTHERN PLEASURES

Maryanne Ashleigh has a woodland garden in the northernmost part of the Northeast.

Here, where we often have frost in late June and early September and where winter temperatures can dip to minus 60 degrees F, tomatoes are a luxury vegetable, not a staple. I plant mainly determinate tomatoes, which I consider much less trouble to maintain than the taller indeterminates. However, in 1984, I did experiment with an indeterminate, *Sweet 100*, which produced clusters of cherry tomatoes all the way up the six-foot vines. These prolific bite-sized tomatoes had a very good taste and were especially appreciated by children. Overall, it was worthwhile planting them, even though the tomatoes did have a tendency to crack. The determinate tomatoes I grew in 1984 were *New Yorker*, *Subarctic Maxi* and *Springset*, all of which produced enormously, considering the adverse weather conditions.

When planting seeds, I follow the Kimberton Hills Biodynamic Calendar, which includes biodynamic gardening instructions and schedules for planting by the moon and planets. Tomatoes are usually sown around the end of March or the beginning of April, depending on the weather conditions at the time. I like to wait until we have a fair amount of sunlight; otherwise, plants become spindly and weak. The seeds are started in 9-by-12-by-2-inch flats, which I fill with last year's compost, brought indoors in fall and mixed with bone meal and blood meal. Once they have sprouted, they are transplanted individually into small cans and finally into larger, recycled containers. The repeated transplanting, each time a little deeper, supposedly stimulates root growth. By the third transplanting, the plants are usually on shelves in a temporary

greenhouse. Here, in order to discourage damping-off disease, plants are watered only in the morning so that they have time to dry off before the greenhouse cools at night. All plants are watered once a week with a fish fertilizer solution that helps produce sturdy, disease-resistant plants to be set out when the time comes.

I plant tomatoes in a small, heated greenhouse, in two large cold frames and in the garden. I could plant in the greenhouse anytime, but to save heating costs, I wait until the regular nightly frosts become occasional frosts, which is usually around the middle of May. Weather permitting, additional tomatoes go into the cold frames a short time later. The cold frames are fairly airtight and are covered with old blankets on cold nights so that light frosts do not affect the tomatoes at all. Outdoor growing of tomatoes is haphazard in many years because of unpredictable, damaging frosts in low locations as late as June 24. I usually wait and plant tomatoes outdoors after the full moon of June, especially if it occurs during the first half of the month, when the danger of frost is the greatest.

I incorporate several wheelbarrows full of compost into each area planted in tomatoes. Under every plant goes a generous handful of bone meal and a small handful of blood meal. To minimize trans-

In a short-season Northeastern garden where "tomatoes are a luxury," Maryanne Ashleigh grows "mainly determinate tomatoes, which I consider much less trouble to maintain than the taller indeterminates."

planting shock, plants are set out on a cloudy day and thoroughly watered with a solution of fish fertilizer. All plants are staked to save space and minimize slug damage, which can be severe when plants are allowed to sprawl on the ground. I prune regularly and trim off many leaves (especially in the greenhouse) to help aerate the plants and discourage fungal diseases. Trimming, which allows more sunlight to fall on the tomatoes, seems to hasten the ripening process. The first week of August, all the flowers that have not set fruit are nipped off to ensure that all the remaining fruits will have time to ripen.

I cannot imagine tomatoes without basil growing nearby, and in 1984, I planted parsley, tomatoes, basil and marigolds in a raised bed outdoors. Basil was planted all around the perimeter, parsley in a row along the center of the bed and tomatoes and marigolds interplanted in two rows parallel to the parsley, the tomato plants two feet apart. In the greenhouse, I plant marigolds between each tomato and purple and green basil in every available space. In cold frames, I leave larger spaces between the tomatoes and fill these later with green peppers.

I find straw mulches very helpful in dry years, but a disadvantage with them in wet summers is that they tend to attract slugs that hide under them all day and munch away on the garden at night. I tried a clear plastic mulch around the tomatoes one year, and it did give good results, but it horrifies me to have to throw away all those disintegrating piles of plastic in the autumn. So until more durable and more ecological mulches are produced, I prefer to minimize their use in my garden.

The only tomato disease I have ever noticed occurred in 1984, when all the tomatoes in the region seemed to be affected by *moisissure des olives*, a grey mold provoked by a cool, wet spring followed by a warm, wet summer. The mold developed on the undersides of the leaves and supposedly floated in the air from one plant to another. I tried to control the disease with a sulphur spray and by cutting off the affected leaves and burning them, but these measures produced absolutely no results. All the tomato plants and leaves were burned in the autumn, and I hope that the conditions that caused the disease will not recur this year. As a precaution in future, I will be spraying my tomato plants with a seaweed foliar spray, which should help the plants combat such fungus diseases. Should they be able to survive the diseases and the frosts for yet another year, I will again freeze bags of tomatoes cooked with zucchini, basil, garlic, beans and peas, a family favorite, and we will have fresh tomatoes, large and small, to eat throughout the summer.

Ashleigh interplanted her tomatoes with marigolds to help discourage pests without chemical pesticides.

TOMATOES IN THE SNOW

Don and Kathy Dill garden in a suburban backyard in the prairie.

Picking tomatoes in the snow is not the best way to harvest a garden, but what else could we do when the first snowfall came in September? After having put months of care into our plants, we found ourselves slogging around in the mud and snow, filling boxes, baskets and pails with green, yellow, pink and red fruit.

There was snow on the ground when we started our garden too. In January, as we sat in front of the fire, we listed and sorted our leftover seeds and decided what we needed to order this year. Then we turned to the seed catalogues and magazine articles to find out what new varieties were available. The hard part for us is limiting ourselves to just the four or six types of tomatoes we can fit in our space-efficient garden. We always include three types of tomatoes: an early variety, a later one and a paste type, choosing the selections of regional seed houses whenever possible.

For our first early-eating tomatoes, we plant *Ping Pong* from T&T Seeds. We find the fruit larger, better-tasting and just as early as the better-known cherry tomato *Tiny Tim*. We grow two or three types of full-sized tomatoes. *Early Girl* has been the earliest-producing one we have tried, and *Early Bush Beefsteak* has been our best-tasting. We generally try one or two others (such as *Blazer* or *Celebrity*) to see how they fare in our conditions. *Royal Chico* is our favourite paste tomato, producing a bountiful supply of relatively early tomatoes that are virtually disease-free.

Seeding usually takes place around the first week of April, about eight weeks before the expected transplant date, although we have sown seeds as early as February 27 and as late as April 24. We start with a few seeds of the full-sized types and then sow the rest of the seeds a week or two later. This way, we have four to six large plants ready to take advantage of an early spring – Don is always eager to jump the gun. We find the large plants do not suffer if they are transplanted into the cold frame.

Seeds are planted in Jiffy 9s (peat pellets available from many garden houses and mail-order seed sources) or in a mixture of one-third each sieved compost, sand and peat or vermiculite. We set the seeded pots on the top of the refrigerator or a radiator to speed germination. When sprouting occurs in four to six days, the seedlings are placed under grow lights in the basement at approximately 60 degrees F. We water the pots from the bottom – that is, pour

23

water into a tray in which the pots sit — to lessen the chances of damping off, which rarely occurs with our seedlings. Two weeks later, when the seedlings have their first true leaves, we transplant them to three-inch peat pots in the same soil mix. If we had enough room, we would start them a bit earlier and transplant all of them into 16-ounce containers (with holes punched in the bottom), as they do outgrow the peat pots before planting-out time. However, with plants crowded under our two banks of grow lights and with tables and windowsills upstairs covered with seedlings of every description, we usually manage to give only the earliest plants the containers; these work well, allowing the roots plenty of room to develop and causing little transplant shock when the plants are put out in the garden.

The tomatoes are kept under the grow lights until the weather is warm enough for them to go out to the cold frame, where they stay until they are transplanted into the garden. Our last frost date is around May 26, and there is still a 25 percent chance of frost on June 3, but we like to get the tomatoes in the ground as soon as possible after the May 24 weekend, provided the soil temperature is above 50 degrees F. Then, we cover the plants if there is a frost warning. Early planting is wise here: it is easier to cover the plants in spring, when they are small, than in fall.

We always save a warm, sunny garden spot for the tomatoes when planning our garden and put a few handfuls of well-rotted manure or compost and a handful of bone meal in each planting hole. Tomatoes in single rows are planted 18 inches apart, while those in the 4-foot-wide raised beds are set at the corners of 24-inch triangles. Large plants are placed on their sides in the planting holes, with only their tops above ground, to minimize transplanting shock. To avoid root damage, stakes are set around the plants at this time. Last year, we tried tomato cages and found that they saved time. We like them and intend to use more in the future.

Our soil is a silty, clay loam, naturally fertile, slightly alkaline but low in organic material. We use raised beds for better drainage and faster warming and for plant protection — it helps keep young children on the paths and off the plants. (Tomatoes are tough, however — one year, three were bitten off almost to the ground by a rambunctious puppy, but they grew back and produced fruit. The fence around the garden was built very soon after this episode.) The soil is nourished with manure, compost, leaves and/or leaf mold. We used to mulch with old hay — less watering, less weeding — and then dug it into the soil in the fall, but we have not mulched for the past two years because we have been trying to keep a slug infestation under control.

The Dills always grow paste-type tomatoes such as Roma VF, *which "make their way into homemade catsup."*

Slugs are really the only pest problem we have with tomatoes. We handpick them and use decaying material in the paths as traps, and if they really get out of control, we buy a pair of ducks, who do an excellent job of eating them as well as fertilizing and weeding.

We plant determinate tomatoes and prune out the suckers on the bottom shoots within about eight inches of the ground for better air movement and slug control. However, two suckers alongside the main stem are left to develop on the full-sized tomatoes, so in essence, there are three stems that are no longer pruned. On the smaller and paste tomatoes, we often do no pruning at all.

During June and July, we try to make sure that the tomatoes receive an inch of water each week, so they will not develop blossom-end rot. We also try to water in the morning so that the plants have a chance to dry before evening, although in our climate, mildew is not a big problem.

We usually start to eat tomatoes around the first of August and often are still eating the last of our fresh garden tomatoes in November. We harvest them as they ripen, until the weather is too cold for them to ripen outdoors – or until it snows – and then we bring them all in, sorting them by color into peach crates that enable us to pick out the ripe ones easily as they mature.

We freeze the majority of our crop as is – 89 pounds in 1984 – for use as tomato sauce and such during the year. Many of our paste tomatoes make their way into homemade catsup. It has been several years since we have used all our frozen tomatoes before the new crop ripens, at which time we may again be picking tomatoes in the snow.

Even if that should happen, tomatoes are still **25**

worth any amount of trouble to us.

LARKWHISTLE BOUNTY

Patrick Lima, co-owner of Larkwhistle Gardens on Ontario's Bruce Peninsula, just across the lake from northern Michigan, relates the tomato-growing techniques that he and John Scanlan have developed.

What we look for in the extensive catalogue listings—at last count, Stokes Seeds alone offered a choice of 78 tomatoes—can be described in three words, "earliness" and "disease resistance." Not for us the beefy *Big Boys* or half-kilo *Braggers* and *Whoppers.* Our own fairly casual trials over 10 years have included a clutch of old favorites, a sampling of the "biggest and best" recent award winners, tomatoes pink, red and yellow, square-shaped and pear-shaped. And always, we have been most pleased with the early, disease-resistant varieties.

For a consistent crop of good-quality, medium-sized fruit as early as the season allows and continuing until frost (and beyond with simple protection), we return annually to *Early Girl, Ultra Girl VFN, Early Cascade VF* and a plant or two of *Sweet 100.* All are staking tomatoes. We have had bumper crops early in the season from the sprawling *Springset VF* and have seen thrifty plants of *Subarctic Maxi,* neat,

ground-hugging nests growing virtually unattended in a cold clay garden, bearing startling quantities of small fruit.

Sometime between April 1 and 10, we fill several dozen four-inch-diameter pots—clay, plastic or pressed fiber—with a mixture that includes roughly four parts garden soil and one part shredded peat moss, well soaked and squeezed. To a bushel of this mix, we add several trowels full of fine bone meal and blend very thoroughly. Our garden soil is light, coarse-textured, sandy loam that has benefited from

10 annual applications of manure, compost and leaves. Gardeners starting with heavy clay or clay loam would do well to incorporate sufficient sand, perlite or vermiculite to lighten the mix. For fewer seedlings, or where overwintering of garden soil is not practical, a sterilized commercial potting soil with an admixture of bone meal provides a weed- and disease-free growing medium.

In each earth-filled pot, we plant three to five tomato seeds toward the centre, no more than one-quarter inch deep. Twelve pots fit a wooden flat, and stacked flats are set on four inverted clay pots sitting directly on the cast-iron surface of the wood stove. This is a most effective way of providing what the books call "gentle bottom heat," which speeds up germination. Be careful not to leave flats unattended over a blazing fire. When the soil surface in the pots is warm to the touch, we remove the flats from the stove and swaddle them in old blankets or sleeping bags to retain the heat.

At the first sign of germination and thereafter, the tomato plants have priority in the sunny space in front of our southeast-facing glass doors. Temperatures here climb to the 70s Fahrenheit when the sun shines and dip below 50 degrees during frosty April nights. The plants thrive. Seedlings are thinned to two and then one per pot as first and second sets of true leaves appear. They need only judicious watering. We allow the soil to become fairly dry between waterings to foster better root development and to minimize the risk of fungal diseases until the time they may be set out in the garden.

But when? The spring weather moves two steps forward and one potentially fatal step back; the gardener goes through minor agonies of indecision. Were tomato plants mobile, I suspect they would promptly pack up and move to Mexico. It is up to the gardener to make these tropical visitors feel at home. If set out too early, plants shiver and succumb to disease or sit still and sulk.

Our solution to the vagaries of a Northern spring is a simple uninsulated cold frame, 2 feet wide and all of 25 feet long, sloping, back to front, from 12 inches to 8 inches. Built in two lengths (for portability) of lumber remnants and covered with eight small storm windows, the "row frame" accommodates our tomato plants during the season of uncertainty and does double or triple duty before and after.

As soon as the snow subsides, windows are fitted over the long frame. Several days of April sunshine are enough to warm the earth to growing temperatures. We seed the frame with a variety of quick-growing, hardy vegetables: spinach, mustard and turnip greens, radishes, leaf lettuce (from seed or, better, transplants begun indoors in mid-March) and some of the Oriental greens. Protected from chilling winds and night frosts, these grow quickly under the glass, and we have harvested spring salad from a frame as early as May 5.

Meanwhile, back at the house, tomato plants are growing apace. On May 20, or thereabouts – some three weeks before we can be certain that frosts are over – we remove, to the salad bowl, dinner-plate-sized patches of greens and young roots every two feet along the length and toward the back (for extra height) of the row frame. Into each planting island just created in a sea of greens, we work a trowel full of bone meal as deeply as possible, then tip husky tomato plants out of their pots and set them into the warm earth several inches deeper than they had been growing. With a solution of fish emulsion mixed half strength, we water copiously into earth wells shaped around each plant to settle the soil around the roots and to provide ready nutrients. Transplanting is accomplished without trauma or setback; plants continue growing unchecked during the variable and often chilly late-spring season. Rewards will come.

The cold frame retains day heat on cold nights, and its covering of window sashes deflects light frosts. Should an unseasonably heavy frost threaten, those old blankets and sleeping bags are pressed into service as frame covers.

By June 10, frame-coddled plants are pushing at the glass. Frame and sash are moved over to another garden bed to receive transplants of cantaloupes and watermelons, other visitors from the tropics that revel in the increased heat during June and early July. The tomatoes are now unprotected, but the weather should remain sufficiently warm to allow them to continue to grow well.

Decisions about pruning and staking tomatoes should have been made when the seeds were ordered. Gardeners who prefer to let their tomatoes roam at will should choose determinate, field-grown-type or bush varieties, which are prolific, space-efficient vines that demand very little care after planting (save for a thick mulch toward the end of June). We grow indeterminate, or staking, tomatoes to make good use of vertical space in an intensive garden, to maximize exposure of fruit to the sun, to minimize rotting of fruit touching the ground and to allow for easier watering, cultivating and harvesting – and, frankly, because one of us simply enjoys fussing with the tomato plants.

At the time that the row frame is removed, we push three stakes deeply into the ground beside and behind each plant – that is, on the north side of the plant. Stakes are 4½-foot long 1½-inch-diameter saplings thinned from the woods, but 1-by-2 lumber, old shovel handles or broomsticks will do.

"We have seen Subarctic Maxi *growing virtually unattended in a cold clay garden, bearing startling quantities of small fruit."*

Short, weak stakes are useless.

We prune to three stems—the main stem, or leader; the first, or lowest, side shoot; and the second side shoot, next up the main stem. Each stem is tied to one of the three stakes. Our reasons are: three branches will provide all the fruit we can use; fruit size increases as the number of branches is restricted—some gardeners opt for two branches, others just one; and because side branches originate near the base of the plant, earth or compost may easily be mounded up around the lower stems to encourage stem rooting and better nutrient uptake.

Once the three stems are established and started on their upward climb, supported against the respective stake with thin strips of soft cloth, pruning consists of removing any and all side shoots sprouting from leaf axils along each stem, *not*, as I have seen, denuding plants of all foliage so that there remains just a forlorn skeleton and clusters of undernourished tomatoes. Sugars stored in the tomatoes—and they are, after all, the succulent *raisons d'être*—are made in the leaves. It is only after fruit has begun to blush that we remove some of the oldest, largest leaves, probably yellowing a bit by now, to admit all the sun to the ripening tomatoes.

The story of pests and diseases is, thankfully, soon told. We have yet to make the acquaintance of tomato hornworms (or *any* tomato bugs) and will forego the pleasure. Disease-resistant varieties prove the best preventive defence against the "troublesome wilts and blights" that tomatoes are heir to.

Uninterrupted growth, a warm environment (be it a frame or a protected sun pocket), balanced organic soil, a few feeds of fish emulsion, intelligent pruning and staking and improved air circulation will all inhibit fungal diseases; even a no-smoking policy near the tomatoes helps—tobacco, a sister Solanaceae, may harbour tomato-afflicting viruses. **29**

It is a maxim of organic culture that well-nourished, strong-growing, lively plants are better able to resist the ravages of insects and diseases. So we have found it. And so we are always assured of thick slices of glistening fruit drizzled with a little olive oil, a generous sprinkling of fresh basil, a few rings of Spanish onion — a salad that is one of the ultimate rewards of home gardening.

MARITIME GARDEN UNDER GLASS

Walter and Maria Gosse tend a 3,200-square-foot plot in Newfoundland.

Our last spring frost in 1984 was on June 25, and it was a killer, reducing the yield of our cherry trees and injuring small plants. So here, where the frost-free season usually runs from about June 15 to early September, tomatoes are almost always grown under shelter. Cherry tomatoes such as *Sweet 100* sometimes do ripen outdoors during our short, cool summers, but in northern Newfoundland, only after an unusually hot season is it possible to harvest any number of ripe, regular-sized tomatoes from plants grown without cover. Because of this, we

grow all our tomatoes in two greenhouses, one solar heated and attached to the house, the other free-standing. In this way, we are able to pick fresh, sun-ripened fruit from June until December.

For several years, the mainstay of our tomato production for both greenhouses has been *Ultra Girl*, although we have found *Earlirouge* equally productive and tasty. In 1984, we also experimented with several other well-known early varieties as well as a couple of new introductions. Of the former, we were most impressed with *Early Girl*, which was a prolific producer of the earliest tomatoes we have ever grown (45 days in the greenhouse). We tried *Better Boy* because of its reputed good flavor and found that it ripened its large, deep red fruit late, even under glass. That was something of an advantage, however, as we were able to enjoy fresh *Better Boy* fruit until December, when some other varieties had finished producing. We will grow it again. *Better Bush*, introduced by Park Seeds in 1984, turned out to be an excellent tomato. It ripened earlier than our *Better Boys* and produced large, delicious fruit on a compact, extremely healthy plant. In fact, we still had one growing in a bucket in our attached greenhouse in December. However, in our region, the 72-day variety could, like *Better Boy*, be grown only under shelter.

Of the small tomatoes, *Sugar Lump* is the best we

The Gosses found that seeds set on the freezer were warmed by the motor and sprouted in about five days.

have ever tasted. We grew one plant in a five-gallon bucket – it was recommended for hanging baskets – and it produced a large, sprawling plant like *Sweet 100* but with better-tasting fruit. We also liked *Patio Prize*, whose fruit was about the size of a plum, with a tart taste, and *Goldie*, a golden cherry tomato we purchased from Park, pretty in salads but not great tasting. *Tiny Tim* is our standard for container growing. We like its sweet-tart taste and prolific growth.

Of the varieties especially developed for greenhouse culture, we are pleased with *Tuckcross*, which is available from Tomato Growers Supply Company. *Tuckcross* is a sturdy, robust variety that produces huge tomatoes, often one or two pounds each. We have been able to keep it growing in our attached greenhouse until late December when, due to ventilation problems (which we are attempting to overcome by planting tomatoes in a center bed rather than next to the glazing), they usually succumb to mildew.

We start our indoor tomatoes around April 7 and

31

those to be grown in the freestanding greenhouse two weeks later. For germination, in the past, we have tried soil cubes, peat pellets, peat pots, flats and empty cottage cheese containers, all of which worked equally well. The only necessary ingredients seem to be: a growing medium, steady heat and moisture. Last year, however, we started our tomatoes in plastic trays that incorporate 20-inch-deep planting furrows. We really liked them because the tomato seedlings were easily removable without our damaging the roots of other seedlings. When we want only one or two plants of a certain type, we like using a peat pellet placed inside a Styrofoam cup to avoid its drying out.

Our starting mix is composed of equal parts of peat, vermiculite and sterile compost. We place the seeded containers, covered with clear plastic punched with a few holes for ventilation (split-open apple bags are great since they are already pre-punched), on top of the refrigerator or the freezer for germination. The heat from the motor provides the right amount of warmth, and in about five days, the seedlings have sprouted. They are then immediately moved into our attached greenhouse, which is still pretty cool in April, but an initial period of cold temperatures is supposed to induce early flowering.

As soon as the true leaves appear — usually four weeks after the seeds were sown — we transplant the

"Better Bush ripened earlier than our Better Boys and produced large, delicious fruit on a compact, healthy plant."

seedlings as deep as possible into two-liter milk cartons, leaving only the top set of leaves showing and removing the lower leaves. This deep planting produces a good root system.

We cut the top off each milk carton and remove the bottom as well, about 1½ inches above the base. The upper section of the carton is then pushed into the base, which we have perforated with three holes. The soil mixture for the cartons consists of equal parts of soil, compost and vermiculite, with some bone meal and ashes added. While they are in the cartons, we fertilize the plants every two weeks with fish emulsion. Then, when we want to transplant the tomatoes into their growing beds, we need only remove the carton bottom and push the plant out from above into a prepared planting hole. When, at times, we have had plants that were too leggy, we have dug a larger hole than usual, like a trench, and laid most of the stem horizontally in the trench, removing any leaves that would otherwise be buried.

The only pests we have in our greenhouses are aphids, which seem to affect the plants most often when there is poor air circulation due to overcrowding. Besides avoiding crowding, the most effective remedy seems to be a soap-solution spray, either the commercial type or a homemade one.

We transplant tomatoes into their permanent beds or containers in the attached greenhouse around May 7 and into the freestanding one around June 15. The soil in both greenhouses has been prepared with generous amounts of compost, ashes, bone meal and a sprinkling of dry manure. After they are planted, we leave two main leaders on the indeterminate plants: the main stem and the first strong sucker that grows below the first set of flowers. We try to remove all other suckers regularly throughout the summer. With strong nylon cord such as macramé cord, we tie each of these two leaders securely to hooks on the greenhouse ceiling, leaving enough slack in the cord so that it can be wound carefully around the stem as it grows. We have found wire cages quite useful for supporting other tomatoes, especially the bush varieties, growing in five-gallon buckets.

We pollinate the tomatoes in the attached greenhouse by gently shaking the flowers every day around noon early in the season. Later in summer, however, a fan and natural ventilation usually take care of it. In the freestanding greenhouse, we leave the pollination job to the bees and the wind, which move freely through the open doors.

By the end of August, we face the unpleasant job of removing the flowers and pinching off the tops of the vines to ensure that fruit already set will mature. After the frost kills the plants in the freestanding greenhouse, we pick all the tomatoes and place them in the basement in shallow cardboard boxes or baskets, covering them loosely with newspaper. We find this a better method than the often recommended wrapping of individual fruits in paper, because it allows us to see at a glance if any tomatoes are getting soft or ripe. From the attached greenhouse, we will continue to pick vine-ripened fruit until the end of the year, when we will again be ordering our seeds for yet another season under glass.

Seeds of Choice

Kinds and Considerations

There are hundreds of different cultivated varieties — properly called cultivars — of tomatoes available to home gardeners. For the beginner facing a seed catalogue or a garden store seed rack, the tomato choice can be a difficult one. And for the experienced gardener, it is all too easy to stay with a familiar standby, rather than risk failure with a new but perhaps better choice.

Fortunately, many tomatoes can easily be crossed off a list of possibilities right at the outset, simply by preference alone. Only you know if you want a cherry tomato or one with pink, low-acid flesh or one that is best suited to canning. Then the choices are further decreased by the days-to-maturity estimation — the approximate number of days from outdoor transplanting to first harvest — which is given in most seed catalogues and which, if known, comes after the cultivar name in the following list, plus a number indicating the catalogue that published the estimate. If different seed companies publish different days-to-maturity estimations, alternates are listed. Gardeners who know the approximate number of days from the last spring frost to the first fall frost in their areas also know the maximum num-

Although they often appear similar, tomato cultivars differ greatly in such important aspects as disease resistance.

35

ber of days to maturity possible for their gardens. The lower the number, the earlier the tomatoes will be ready to harvest.

Other considerations include the preference for hybrid or nonhybrid – the latter tend to have less expensive seed, and their fruit can be used as a source of next year's seeds, according to the instructions on page 118. Also, gardeners can choose a determinate – a bush-type tomato that is adequately supported in a cage, and may even be left to sprawl, and produces its crops over a relatively short time span – or an indeterminate, a tall tomato that should be pruned and staked and will probably keep producing fruit until frost. The letter **V** after the variety name means plants are resistant to verticillium wilt; **F** indicates resistance to fusariam wilt; and **N** means the plant is resistant to nematode attack.

Best Tomatoes for Northern Gardeners

Within each cultivar description, the numbers listed refer to seed companies selling that tomato. The seed companies are listed in *Sources,* **page 50.**

EARLY

Alicante (*Suttons Alicante*) 68 days **(21)**
This British indeterminate produces "an excellent crop of medium-large fleshy fruits of fine flavour," according to Suttons Seeds of England. **16, 21**

Beefeater VFN (*Italian Beefsteak*) 60 days **(17)**
For such an early cultivar, this disease-resistant, determinate hybrid has unusually large fruit. Weighing as much as two pounds, they are reported by Stokes to have "outstanding taste." **17**

Bush Beefsteak 62 days **(17)**
A popular home-garden choice that has fleshy,

SUB-ARCTICS

A few seasons have passed since my first northern garden, and this experience has taught me that we are not entirely at the mercy of temperamental weather. Now when I choose seeds, I check maturity period first and use the bulk of my garden space for short-season-variety garden basics. With tomatoes, maturity periods are especially important. The tomatoes I tried to grow the first year were supposed to give me big, juicy, scrumptious fruit. At season's end, I had to carry all the good-sized green tomatoes into the house to ripen. Many were too small to bother with — they would have shriveled to raisins. To watch tomatoes grow very slowly all summer and not be able to put one tomato into a salad bowl — that is frustration. *Sub-Arctic* tomatoes are not as good tasting as 75-day big tomatoes, but now I'm inclined to choose varieties I am sure will succeed. To sow for flavor only is to go for Sunday best. It is fun to have fancy clothes on a homestead, but overalls we need.

— *Teruko Low*

eight-ounce, mild-flavored fruit with few seeds but has been surpassed in earliness and quality by some of the newer nonhybrid, determinate beefsteak cultivars such as *Basketvee* or *Moira*. **17, 18, 23**

Coldset 65 days **(5)**
The only standard cultivar that can be dependably seeded directly outdoors in soil as cool as 50 degrees F, *Coldset* is especially valuable where summers are cool, as it also sets fruit well in low temperatures. Juicy, four-ounce fruits are borne on nonhybrid, determinate vines. **1, 5, 17, 23**

Earlibright 60 days **(17)**, 63 days **(8)**
Deep red, sweet and tasty, with four-to-six-ounce crack-resistant fruit. Developed in Ontario, it sets fruit well in cool, wet weather. Nonhybrid determinate. **8, 17, 23**

Earlirouge 63 days **(17)**, 66 days **(8)**
Johnny's claims this verticillium-wilt-resistant, Ontario nonhybrid determinate is "of better quality than *Springset, New Yorker* and others in that early-maturity" range. Produces round, red, sweet and delicious, six-ounce fruits. **1, 8, 17, 23**

Early Cascade VFN 66 days **(8)**
Johnny's calls it "the best early staking tomato for

home gardens." This American hybrid produces medium-small, round, red, crack-resistant fruit with delicious flavor and has disease resistance. Indeterminate vines. **5, 7, 8, 20, 22, 23, 24, 26**

Early Girl 54 days **(11)**
Called "the best early hybrid" by Mountain Seed & Nursery, this indeterminate produces fairly large, red, round or flattened, slightly acid fruit until fall. **2, 5, 7, 10, 11, 14, 22, 23, 25**

Fantastic 65 days **(24)**
This hybrid tomato produces very tasty medium-sized, round, red fruits on vigorous vines that must be staked. **9, 11, 12, 17, 18, 20, 22, 23, 24**

Florida Petite 52 days **(17)**
Earliest of the cherry tomatoes in some tests, this prolific producer of one-inch or larger, round, red fruits on small, determinate plants is well suited to four-inch or larger pots or baskets. Nonhybrid. **17, 21, 22, 23**

Gardener's Delight (*Sugar Lump*) 68 days **(8)**
An indeterminate, nonhybrid cherry tomato with fruit that may be too sweet for some. This German cultivar develops heavy crops of medium-sized fruit on long, vigorous vines. **2, 8, 11, 13, 21, 22, 23**

Gem State 58 days **(8)**
Especially recommended for containers and small gardens, *Gem State* has an upright, sturdy stem that needs no support. The nonhybrid, red, flavorful fruit is about two ounces. **8, 10, 23**

Glacier 45 days **(15)**
A 1985 introduction from Siberia Seeds, who says that this determinate, nonhybrid tomato may be the same as *Imur Prior Beta*. Prolific producer of red fruit of approximately two-ounce size. **15**

Golden Delight 65 days **(17)**
Low-acid, three- or four-ounce fruits are bright yellow when ripe. Nonhybrid, determinate. **17, 23**

Ida Gold 59 days **(8)**
The earliest of the low-acid, golden-fruited tomatoes, this Idaho determinate was developed especially for Northern growers. Fruits are nonhybrid and weigh about two ounces. **8, 10, 13, 23**

Italian Beefsteak (see *Beefeater VFN*)

The Juice 72 days **(22)**
Determinate hybrid that produces especially juicy, six-to-eight-ounce fruits. **22**

Earlibright

Manitoba
Early, bright red, nonhybrid, firm fruit with superior flavor is borne on determinate plants. **17, 23**

Moira 66 days (17), 73 days (8)
Determinate, dwarf bush beefsteak produced in Ontario. The nonhybrid fruits are bright red and weigh about six ounces. Tomato breeder Edward Lowden notes: "Many in the harsher climates, who grow chiefly the *Sub-Arctics* and other very early tomatoes, have had success with *Moira.*" **8, 17, 23**

New Yorker V 60 days (25), 66 days (22)
The Vermont Bean Seed Company calls this "our earliest tomato. Very early and compact. Grows well caged, setting fruit under cool weather conditions. Ideal for growth in New England. The determinate plant shows concentrated sets of 3 to 5 oz. bright red deep globed fruits." **2, 6, 20, 22, 23, 25**

Patio F 50 days (17), 70 days (11)
Strong, upright stems that need no staking make the plant well suited to containers. Grows about two feet tall and produces four-ounce hybrid fruit "of the highest quality," says Park. **11, 17, 22, 23, 24, 25**

Patio Prize VFN 52 days (17), 67 days (11)
Similar to *Patio F*, but a little later, with slightly

39

larger, five-ounce fruit. Hybrid. **11, 12, 17, 22, 23**

Ping Pong 50 days (18)
T&T Seeds describes this as "compact bushy plants loaded with small ping pong size fruit with a tender skin. Holds ripe fruit and resists splitting. Excellent sweet flavour." **18** (13 carries a yellow variety, which produces "glowing golden balls.")

Pixie 52 days (2)
Hybrid, stiff-stemmed, upright determinate that produces smooth, meaty 1¾-ounce fruits. Well suited to hydroponics and pots. **2, 10, 16, 21, 22, 23**

Rocket 50 days (17)
Although it is not a heavy bearer, Mountain Seed & Nursery says that *Rocket* has "the best fruit quality" of the extra-earlies. Sweet, tasty, nonhybrid fruits average just 1¼ inches across and are borne on determinate plants. **10, 15, 17, 23**

Scotia 60 days (17)
A Nova Scotia nonhybrid determinate that sets slightly green-shouldered, red fruit well at low temperatures. **17, 23**

40   Siberia 48 to 60 days (15)

SEEDY SKEPTICISM

There is no doubt that something can be gained in the way of early maturity by annually selecting for seed the first well-formed tomatoes that ripen and sowing only such seed. Every year, some new sort is advertised which is to be from 10 to 30 days earlier than any other, but it never turns out to be any earlier than those that have been in cultivation for years. We advise every tomato grower to save his own seed from his earliest good specimens and let the "greenhorns" buy the wonderful novelties.
— *D.W. Beadle*
The Canadian Fruit, Flower & Kitchen Gardener, 1872

Nonhybrid fruit of approximately four-ounce size on determinate, cold-resistant plants. Suitable for fresh use or processing. **1, 15**

Small Fry VFN 68 days (6)
More disease-resistant than most cherry tomatoes, this hybrid determinate produces inch-wide, uniform, tasty red fruit. **6, 11, 17, 20, 22, 23**

Springset VF 62 days (17)
Heavy yields of early, delicious, beefsteak-type hybrid tomatoes on determinate plants. Sets well in cool weather, although the 6½-ounce fruit is somewhat soft and susceptible to cracking. **12, 15, 17, 22, 23, 24**

Sprint 59 days (8)
Johnny's Selected Seeds describes this as an upright indeterminate, which has green shoulders and a tendency to crack but which produces unusually sweet, disease-free fruit for such an early cultivar. The nonhybrid fruits are small, round and weigh about two ounces. **8**

Starfire 56 days (17)
Developed at Morden, Manitoba, this nonhybrid produces large yields of brilliant red, almost half-pound, thick-walled, low-acid fruit on foot-high determinate plants. Stokes offers "re-selected" seed for fruit averaging eight ounces. **17, 18, 23**

Stokesalaska 55 days (17)
Stokes recommends this prolific producer of mild, sweet-tasting, small red fruit for Northern tubs and stakes. Nonhybrid. **17, 23**

Stupice
Abundant Life describes this Czechoslovakian red-fruited nonhybrid as "a remarkable plant, one of the earliest tomatoes known and yet a good yielder with excellent flavor . . . . Rave reviews from Ontario to California." **1**

BUSH OR STAKING

Bush, or determinate, plants are compact, producing many comparatively short branches, or laterals. They are not meant to be staked, though this is sometimes done in wet areas to keep the fruit away from the ground.

While the ripening of first fruit is no earlier than on staking types, a greater total yield of fruit is concentrated in the early period.

Staking, or indeterminate, plants are generally large and vigorous, with fruit trusses widely spaced. The plants will cover a large area unless staked and pruned. Although the first truss may set early, each of the ensuing trusses are successively later.

Tomatoes in the Home Garden

Sub-Arctic Maxi 48 days (**17**), 62 days (**8**)
With the largest fruit (at about 2½ or 3 ounces) of the *Sub-Arctics*, this small determinate is also the most flavorful, although it does not compete in flavor with many later-maturing cultivars. It is susceptible to early blight. **7, 8, 10, 12, 15, 17, 23**

Sub-Arctic Plenty 58 days (**8**)
A prolific nonhybrid producer of 1½-to-2-ounce fruits on upright stems. **5, 8, 10, 21, 23**

Sugar Lump (see *Gardener's Delight*)

Suttons Alicante (see *Alicante*)

Sweet 100 60 days (**17**), 65 days (**24**)
Produces very heavy crops of extremely sweet, round, red, inch-wide cherry tomatoes on indeterminate, grapelike vines. **2, 5, 6, 7, 10, 11, 12, 14, 17, 21, 22, 23, 24, 25**

Swift 54 days (**17**)
A Northern favorite, thanks to its ability to set fruit well at low temperatures. Developed in Saskatchewan, this nonhybrid determinate produces small, round, deep red fruit that ripens almost simultaneously. **17, 23**

Starfire

Stokes Seeds

Tiny Tim 45 days (17), 60 days (8)
A nonhybrid, dwarf determinate long popular for its small, sturdy, upright plants and prolific bearing of round, red, relatively large cherry fruit that is, however, somewhat acidic and thick-skinned. Good for a pot in a sunny window. **2, 4, 8, 11, 12, 13, 17, 18, 22, 23, 25**

Toy Boy VF 55 days (17)
Early producer of plenty of round, red "candy sweet" 1½-inch-wide fruits on two-foot-tall, hybrid, determinate, cascading plants, especially recommended for containers. **11, 14, 17, 22, 23**

Ultra Girl VFN 62 days (17)
Disease-resistant hybrid with firm, seven-to-nine-ounce fruits that are red and lack green shoulders. Semideterminate, so it should be staked or caged. **17, 23**

Whippersnapper 52 days (8)
A nonhybrid determinate developed by Johnny's Selected Seeds and recommended for hanging planters and salad bars. Oval, pinkish red fruits are about an inch long and have "plenty of flavor." **8, 23**

MIDSEASON

Basketvee 70 days (17)
On determinate vines, this Ontario-bred nonhybrid produces nine-ounce, meaty beefsteak fruits with good color and flavor. **17, 23**

Bellstar 70 days (17), 74 days (8)
Plum-type fruits that, at four to six ounces, are nearly twice as large as those from other plants. This is a compact, nonhybrid determinate; Johnny's notes it is highly rated in processing tests and that its good flavor allows it to double as a salad tomato. Stokes recommends it for containers. **8, 17, 23**

Better Boy VFN 72 days (17)
One-pound-sized hybrid, sweet, beefsteak-type fruit on disease-resistant, indeterminate vines. **2, 3, 11, 12, 14, 17, 22, 23, 24, 25, 26**

Blazer VF
This hybrid tomato, according to The Tomato Seed Company, has "red, determinate, concentrated set, uniform fruit," and they class it as large, in the ½-to-¾-pound range. **23**

THE STALWART FOUR

After selecting early-maturing, disease-resistant plants, I try several different cultivars every year in my northeastern garden. I have tried about 20 during the past five or six years and have come up with four dependable, prolific selections significantly different from one another: *Sweet 100, Yellow Pear, Early Cascade* and *Ultra Girl.*

Trained on a south-facing wall, my *Sweet 100*s have grown all the way to the roofline of my two-story house. Furthermore, they begin to produce fruit early: I picked my first *Sweet 100* tomatoes on June 28, June 20 and June 27 in 1981, 1982 and 1983, respectively.

Yellow Pear is, as the name implies, a pear-shaped tomato. But unlike most pear-shaped paste tomatoes, it is less than an inch long and is bright yellow, adding a colorful touch to salads. Like *Sweet 100, Yellow Pear* is indeterminate, producing fruit continuously until fall, but it suffers somewhat from virus wilts and cannot measure up to the flavor of my other favorites.

Early Cascade is my favorite slicing and lunch-box tomato. If given an early start and some frost protection, it will match *Sweet 100* in bearing from late June to early October on indeterminate vines. I have picked my first *Early Cascade*s on June 16, June 20 and June 23 for the last three years. The fruit is meaty and two or three inches across, not large but perfect for eating whole or quartering into a salad and adequate for slicing into sandwiches.

To obtain a large quantity of fruit in a relatively short period of time for freezing and preserving, I count on the wonderfully reliable *Ultra Girl*, a main-crop semideterminate – a plant with some features of both determinates and indeterminates. The hybrid plants, which are resistant to virus wilts, become loaded with tomatoes that develop fairly late but mature quickly to almost half-pound size. The uniformly sized, delicious red fruit has never been deformed by blossom-end rot or catfacing in my garden. This year, with a late, cold spring, I did not set my *Ultra Girl* tomatoes into the garden until June 10. Even so, I started picking ripe fruit on August 2, about 50 days later – almost a week before Stokes Seeds' estimated maturity date of 56 days. The plants were eight weeks old when transplanted and had been grown in individual containers, so they had had a particularly good start.

— *George Bushell*

Bonny Best 78 days (8)

An old, disease-susceptible, indeterminate nonhybrid that produces fruits of varying shape and size but still popular because of its generally good flavor. Stokes sells "super-standard" seed but includes the cultivar only "for sentimental purposes." **1, 3, 8, 12, 13, 17, 22, 23**

Celebrity VFNT 70 days (17), 75 days (8)

The 1984 All-America award-winning determinate hybrid, resistant to many diseases, is a reliable producer of 7-to-12-ounce bright red, firm fruit with a mild flavor. **2, 6, 8, 11, 12, 14, 15, 17, 18, 21, 22, 23, 24**

Floramerica VF 76 days (24)

A hybrid, determinate, All-America Selections winner, *Floramerica* is resistant to 15 diseases and is capable of producing 8-to-12-ounce, red, round fruit under varying weather and soil conditions. Mild flavor. **2, 6, 11, 12, 17, 22, 23, 24, 25, 26**

Nova 65 days (17), 72 days (8)

A relatively early paste type that is a cross between *New Yorker* and *Roma* from Geneva, New York. Elongated, red, firm, two-ounce fruits are produced on wilt-resistant, compact, determinate vines. Nonhybrid. **1, 8, 15, 17, 23**

Pik Red (*Red Pak*) 70 days (7)

Ed Hume describes this hybrid, determinate, beefsteak type as his own favorite "that ripens consistently in a cool climate. Large tomatoes can weigh up to two pounds each. Fruit is firm, juicy, solid red." **6, 7, 23**

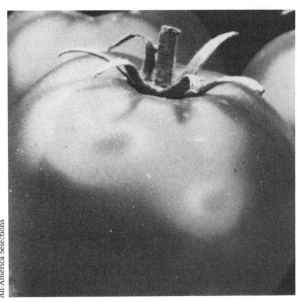

All-America Selections

Celebrity

Pink Girl 76 days (24)
A low-acid, pink indeterminate with good tolerance to fusarium and verticillium wilts and excellent tolerance to cracking. Fruits average about one-half pound. Hybrid. **2, 5, 6, 17, 22, 23, 24**

Quinte (*Easy Peel*) 70 days (17)
Notable because its skin peels off like that of a peach, without blanching, shortcutting the tomato sauce-making process. Firm, red fruit is approximately one-half pound. **17, 23**

Red Express 238 74 days (8)
This is something of an earlier *Long Keeper*, valued for its excellent shelf life. The flavorful red fruits weigh 8 to 10 ounces apiece and are borne on hybrid, determinate plants resistant to verticillium and fusarium wilts, nematodes. **8, 11, 22, 23**

Red Pak (see *Pik Red*)

Royal Chico VFN 70 days (18) 80 days (24)
According to The Tomato Seed Company, this determinate, 3½ oz. pear-shaped tomato is "not for short season northern gardeners." Tomato Growers Supply Company and others, however, call it "outstanding for paste or canning," and many gardeners have had success with it. **5, 18, 22, 23, 24**

Tuckcross 520 F 74 days (22)
"One of the best varieties for greenhouse growing," says Tomato Growers Supply Company. This indeterminate produces a 7 oz. fruit that is smooth and bright red. **22**

Ultra Boy VFN 72 days (17)
Stokes calls this "the best of the extralarge-fruited 'Boy' series." Hybrid, disease-resistant indeterminate with globe fruit averaging over one pound. **17, 21, 23**

Veepick 73 days (17)
This oblong-shaped member of the "vee" series of Ontario-bred nonhybrids was described by tomato breeder Edward Lowden as "outstandingly distinct. It is well named, for the fruits show up for picking far more than any tomato I know. It is very solid, and I did not see a blemish in the whole patch." **17, 23**

Veeroma VF 72 days (17)
Verticillium- and fusarium-resistant nonhybrid cultivar with pear-shaped, crack-resistant fruit that is excellent for canning. **17, 23**

Burpee's Big Boy VFN

LATE

Beefmaster VFN 80 days (12)

For gardeners with a long season, these deep, oblate fruits, which weigh as much as two pounds apiece, bring compliments. Fruits are delicious, round and red. **5, 6, 11, 12, 22, 23**

Burgess Stuffing 78 days (22)

With an almost completely hollow core, as in a green pepper, this unusual red tomato was developed especially for stuffing. Nonhybrid. **22**

Burpee's Big Boy VFN 78 days (17)

Smooth, red, good-flavored, low-acid fruits that weigh as much as one pound each, on vigorous, hybrid, indeterminate vines. **2, 3, 5, 11, 12, 16, 17, 23, 24, 26**

Caro Rich 80 days (17)

Notable because of its very high vitamin A content, the four-to-six-ounce fruit has a rich, deep golden color and very low acidity. Irregular, beefsteak-type fruits. **17, 23**

Golden Boy 78 days (24)

A hybrid indeterminate whose large fruits are renowned for their mild, low-acid flavor. **12, 22, 23, 24, 25**

Harvestvee VF 75 days (17)

Described by Stokes as "the best variety for home-garden canning," *Harvestvee* is nevertheless not a plum tomato but can be used in salads, producing 8½-ounce beefsteak-type, almost seedless fruit on nonhybrid determinate vines. **17, 23**

Lemon Boy VFN 70 days (11), 82 days (8)
Rather than the usual gold, these half-pound, meaty fruits are bright yellow and said to be more flavorful than the golden types. This first yellow member of the extra-large-fruited "Boy" series is an indeterminate hybrid. **5, 6, 8, 11, 18, 22, 23, 25**

Long Keeper 78 days (12)
Slow to ripen, this tomato is unusual in its ability to be stored indoors at cool temperatures for 6 to 12 weeks after harvesting. The fruit is juicy and golden but does not compare in flavor with other late tomatoes. Harvest fruits when partially ripe, before frost. **1, 2, 12, 18, 22**

Ponderosa (*Pink Beefsteak, Pink Ponderosa*)
83 days (24)
Fruits that average 14 ounces but may exceed two pounds, have beefsteak shape but are pinkish or purplish in color and have mild, low-acid, solid flesh. Twilley's sells an "improved" strain of this determinate. **3, 6, 13, 17, 22, 23, 24, 25**

Roma VF 76 days (24)
A nonhybrid, prolific and disease-resistant producer of plum-type tomatoes on a compact, determinate plant. **2, 3, 5, 6, 7, 9, 11, 14, 17, 22, 23, 24, 25, 26**

Long Keeper

W. Atlee Burpee Co.

Vendor VF 76 days (8)

The standard choice for home greenhouses now has disease resistance that makes it suitable for outdoor, staked growth as well. Round, bright red fruit four to eight ounces is produced on indeterminate vines. **8.** *Vendor VFT* is sold by **23.** *Vendor* without the VF rating is sold by **17.**

White Beauty 85 days (22)

A conversation piece that is also valued by gardeners with little tolerance to tomato acids, this low-acid cultivar produces big fruits that are white when ripe. **4, 5, 13, 22, 23**

Yellow Pear 75 days (7)

Unusual for its small, yellow, pear-shaped fruit, this is a popular nonhybrid determinate. **1, 2, 4, 5, 6, 7, 9, 12, 13, 17, 22, 23**

FRUITING PHOENIX

I would like to encourage cold-climate gardeners by saying that tomato plants are not as frost-sensitive as we have been led to believe. We have had tomato plants blackened by overnight frost one year and blackened and shredded by hail another year. Both these events occurred in the first week of June, but by July, these plants had completely recovered, and we still had ripe tomatoes, though the size of the crop was reduced.

Also, one fall, we were caught with an overnight frost in October. The plants were black except for the odd branch that was still green near the house wall. I decided not to pull up the plants and later in November picked ripe, red tomatoes (mostly *Sweet 100*s, but a few larger tomatoes) from these branches.

— *E. Lozowski*

SUCCESS IS HOLLOW

*Burgess Stuffing*s are indeterminate plants that keep growing and bearing until frost cuts them down, usually in September here in Wisconsin. We do not prune our tomatoes, so the *Stuffing*s climb up and over the sides of the cages. We have found them less prone to blossom-end rot or cracking after a heavy rain than other tomatoes, and *Stuffing*s are also resistant to verticillium and fusarium wilts and nematodes. This is not an early tomato, however, taking about 78 days to mature after transplanting.

The fruits are fist-sized, smooth-skinned and blocky, easily mistaken for green peppers. Like peppers, they are hollow. Tap a *Stuffing*, and it sounds like a tiny drum with skin that should be keyed down. And like peppers, they make fine little cups into which summer salads or hot winter dishes may be packed. Alberta Nurseries and Seeds, which advertises the *Burgess Stuffing* in its "gourmet center," notes, too, that "the vertical ribs on its exterior are highly decorative when prepared for the table."

— *Michael Goc*
Friendship, Wisconsin

SOURCES

1
ABUNDANT LIFE SEED FOUNDATION
Box 772
Port Townsend, Washington 98368
Catalogue alone $1; catalogue plus newsletters $4.

2
W. ATLEE BURPEE COMPANY
300 Park Avenue
Warminster, Pennsylvania 18974
Catalogue free.

3
DeGIORGI COMPANY, INC.
P.O. Box 413
Council Bluffs, Iowa 51502
Catalogue $1.

4
GLECKLER'S SEEDMEN
Metamora, Ohio 43540
Catalogue free.

5
GURNEY'S SEED & NURSERY CO.
2551 Page Street

Yankton, South Dakota 57079
Catalogue free.

6
HARRIS MORAN SEED COMPANY
3670 Buffalo Road
Rochester, New York 14624
Catalogue free.

7
ED HUME SEEDS, INC.
P.O. Box 1450
Kent, Washington 98032
Catalogue free.

8
JOHNNY'S SELECTED SEEDS
299 Foss Hill Road
Albion, Maine 04910
Catalogue free.

9
LE MARCHE SEEDS INTERNATIONAL
P.O. Box 566
Dixon, California 95620
Catalogue $2.

10
MOUNTAIN SEED AND NURSERY
P.O. Box 9107
Moscow, Idaho 83843

Catalogue $1, refundable with first order.

11
GEO. W. PARK SEED COMPANY, INC.
Greenwood, South Carolina 29647
Catalogue free.

12
PINETREE GARDEN SEEDS
Route 100
New Gloucester, Maine 04260
Catalogue free.

13
SEEDS BLUM
Idaho City Stage
Boise, Idaho 83706
Catalogue $2.

14
SHOESTRING SEEDS
P.O. Box 2261
Martinsville, Virginia 24113
Catalogue free.

15
SIBERIA SEEDS
Box 2026
Sweetgrass, Montana 59484
Catalogue 50 cents, or send a self-addressed, stamped
envelope.

16
SMITHS OF HAZLEHEAD
Aberdeen, Scotland AB9 2QU
Catalogue $2.

17
STOKES SEEDS LTD.
1436 Stokes Building
Buffalo, New York 14240
Catalogue free.

18
T&T SEEDS
P.O. Box 1710
Winnipeg, Manitoba R3C 3P6
Catalogue 75 cents.

19
TATER-MATER SEEDS
Thomas P. Wagner
R.R. 2
Wathena, Kansas 66090
Catalogue free; all varieties listed are experimental –
intriguing to tomato adventurers.

20
TERRITORIAL SEED CO.
Box 27
Lorane, Oregon 97451
Catalogue free to gardeners west of the Cascade
Mountains; not available elsewhere.

21
THOMPSON & MORGAN, INC.
Box 1308
Jackson, New Jersey 08527
Catalogue free.

22
TOMATO GROWERS SUPPLY COMPANY
P.O. Box 2237
Fort Myers, Florida 33902
Catalogue free.

23
THE TOMATO SEED COMPANY, INC.
P.O. Box 323
Metuchen, New Jersey 08840
Catalogue free.

24
TWILLEY SEED CO. INC.
P.O. Box 65
Trevose, Pennsylvania 19047
Catalogue free.

25
VERMONT BEAN SEED CO.
Bomoseen, Vermont 05732
Catalogue free.

26
WYATT-QUARLES SEED CO.
Box 739
Garner, North Carolina 27529
Catalogue free.

Ontario Ministry of Agriculture and Food

An elaborate system of glass covers provides essential spring frost protection to a field of Ontario tomatoes.

Starting Right

The Care and Feeding of Young Tomatoes

I f the enormous potential in a packet of tomato seeds seems daunting to the beginning gardener, it is a challenge to even the most experienced. First, all gardens larger than a balcony pot or greenhouse bench must be fertile, weeded and in good condition before they receive the young tomato seedlings — as many as 15 plants per person if they will be used for a year's supply of tomato sauce, catsup and such. Then, long before they are planted outdoors in that well-prepared garden, the seedlings must be care-fully tended, never exposed to temperatures too high or too low, never allowed to become too wet or too dry for too long and always exposed to as much sunlight as possible. Even purchased transplants need proper handling before they confront the elements outdoors. Once in the garden, tomatoes need continuing care and, perhaps most important, protection from the most damaging of Northern dangers, spring frost.

— JB

Already promising a bountiful harvest, these healthy, flat-grown tomatoes are the evidence of careful tending.

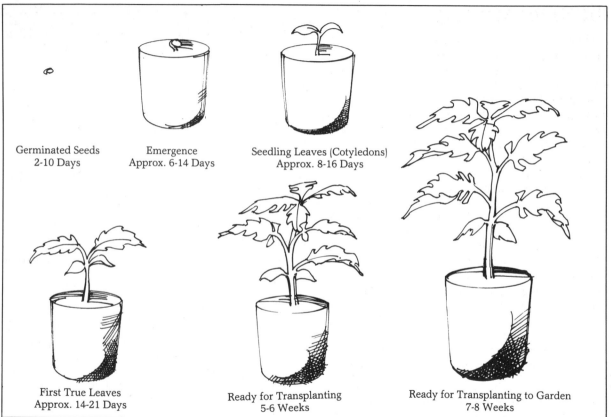

Germinated Seeds
2-10 Days

Emergence
Approx. 6-14 Days

Seedling Leaves (Cotyledons)
Approx. 8-16 Days

First True Leaves
Approx. 14-21 Days

Ready for Transplanting
5-6 Weeks

Ready for Transplanting to Garden
7-8 Weeks

Ian S.R. Grainge

PIONEER ADVICE

Those who desire to raise a few plants for home use can start them in the house by sowing the seed in a box filled with good, rich soil, and keeping it in a warm kitchen window. The kitchen is the best room in the house for plants, because the air is filled with moisture from the water that is kept almost constantly on the stove in the various operations of cooking and washing that are carried on there. When the plants are fairly started, if they stand too thick, enough may be pulled out to give the remainder sufficient room; and if these are needed, they may be planted in another box of earth, kept shaded and well watered for a few days, when they will have taken fresh root and may be set in the light. As often as the weather will permit, the boxes should be set outside the window, where they will get the sun and air and be sheltered from chilly winds, not forgetting to take them in if the weather should suddenly change to a colder temperature and always at night. In this way, strong, stocky and healthy plants can be grown, which may be set out and sheltered with boards for a time, until the weather becomes warm enough to put them in the open garden.

— *D.W. Beadle*
**Canadian Fruit, Flower & Kitchen Gardener,
1872**

LET THERE BE LIGHT

The kitchen windowsill, a favorite spot, may give adequate sunlight to seedlings if it faces south, but remember that high temperatures of 80 degrees F or more may promote "leggy" growth. Pinch back the growing tips if your plants show signs of becoming spindly. Supplemental light from fluorescent lamps, particularly in combination with ordinary incandescent bulbs, promotes good growth. Seedlings should not be subjected to more than 16 hours of light a day, however, as continuous light may cause injury.

Growing Garden Tomatoes

THE CARE AND FEEDING OF YOUNG TOMATOES

Seed pre-germination helps get the crop off to a good start. It is much easier to keep a small container of seeds warm and damp than it is to maintain proper germination temperatures for entire soil-filled flats or containers. And in this way, only viable seeds are planted.

57

Germination should begin about two full months before the last predicted frost in the gardener's area. With warm water, moisten a piece of paper or cloth toweling, and place it on the bottom of a plastic container. Then cover it with a single layer of tomato seeds. Sprout as many seeds as you want plants, adding 10 percent to compensate for germination failures. Cover the seeds with another wet towel, close the container, and place it in a warm spot — the best germination temperature is about 75 to 85 degrees F. Check the seeds occasionally to make sure the toweling has not dried. Within a week, the small root emerging from each seed should be sufficiently long — about one-quarter inch — to allow the seed to be planted. Leave ungerminated seeds longer, removing any that appear shadowed, because they will not sprout.

Now fill a selection of containers perforated for drainage — flats, milk cartons, Styrofoam or paper drinking cups, peat pellets or pots — with a dampened growing medium such as sterilized compost or garden soil mixed half and half with vermiculite or with a commercial potting mix. A sterile medium is especially important, since damping off, a fungus disease that is always a threat to seedlings, is even more likely than usual to occur during the "cold treatment" that follows. Sterilized soil mixtures are readily available, but gardeners who wish to sterilize their own potting soil should spread it no more than four inches deep in baking trays and bake it for about 90 minutes at 300 degrees F. Once cool, it is ready to use. Each germinated seed is placed about one-quarter inch deep in the potting mix and is allowed about four square inches of growing space.

Keep the growing medium damp and fairly warm until the green shoots appear, and then place the plants in a sunny spot, such as a south-facing window, a greenhouse or under grow lights, turning the pots every few days to keep the plants growing straight. Once the first true serrated leaves appear, the cold treatment, an optional method aimed at encouraging an especially large crop of early tomatoes, begins.

Place the young plants in a cool place, 50 to 55 degrees F, every night for three weeks, allowing them as much sunlight as possible during the day. After three weeks, maintain warm temperatures — at least 60 to 65 degrees — both day and night, if possible. The cold treatment increases the number of flowers while decreasing the number of leaves on the first clusters. It does not influence the setting of fruit. If, after the plants are set out in the garden, night temperatures are suitable for fruit setting, a greater number of flowers will set fruit on the first clusters than would otherwise have been the case. If, however, night temperatures are low (53 to 56 degrees) at bloom time, the pollen of most commercial varieties will not germinate, and the fruit will not set. Some varieties, though, have especially good cold-setting ability (including *Basketvee, Coldset* and *Swift*).

About three weeks before the last predicted spring frost, transplant the tomatoes into larger containers—half-gallon milk cartons, plant pots or juice cans—one plant to a container. At this point, any good garden soil or compost, with a little vermiculite mixed in, can be used. Sterilization is not necessary. Plant the tomato, complete with the root ball removed from its initial container, as deeply as the first true leaves. The cotyledons will be covered in soil. Water it and set it back on the sunny windowsill. A week before the last frost date, begin hardening the plants off by taking them outdoors on a warm day, leaving them for an hour in a calm, shaded place. Every day, leave the plants out a little longer, until they remain outdoors all day and all night as well. Take them in, of course, if frost is predicted.

— JB

OUTDOOR PROTECTION

The timing of both hardening off and planting will depend on the weather during any particular spring. If days are warm and sunny and the nights are not frosty, move the schedule ahead so that the plants go into the garden before the last predicted frost date. If a frost warning does occur, the plants can easily be covered in the evening; it is much more convenient to protect such small plants than to cover huge bushes in fall.

Allowing about two feet in each direction per plant, dig a hole of sufficient size to accommodate both its present root ball and much of its stem as well. Place the root ball and stem parallel to, but just under, the soil surface to ensure that the roots do not descend into really cool soil for a week or so. Fill the hole with compost, and then insert a ring of paper or cardboard into the soil, encircling each stem to fend off cutworms.

If stakes are to be inserted, do it now while the roots can be easily avoided. Those who wish to keep their determinates, or bush, tomatoes off the ground should either cage them or tie several branches to one stake.

Most gardeners who grow determinates simply choose to let them sprawl. Whether the plants are to be supported or not, apply a mulch to the tomato garden. Plastic, either clear or black, can be placed around the plants as soon as they are in the garden and will help warm the soil while keeping the area weed-free.

If the gardener decides, instead, to use an organic mulch, such as lawn clippings, straw or newspaper, this should not be applied for about two weeks, until the soil has warmed considerably. Until then, keep the weeds under control. Such an organic mulch is beneficial to the garden, adding nutrients to the soil while controlling weeds and keeping the fruit clean.

While the plants are small, any kind of cloche will provide a greenhouse environment, protecting the plants from nighttime frosts and enhancing daytime temperatures. Such a cover, placed over individual plants or over rows of plants, should allow sunlight to enter while holding warmth inside and yet must provide for adequate ventilation. Tepees of clear plastic, a lean-to made with an old storm window or commercial hot caps or cloches will encourage the growth of warmth-loving plants such as tomatoes. Remove covers when summer temperatures have stabilized.

— JB

SETTING PLANTS OUT

Set plants that are in peat pots directly into the soil without removing pots. To allow the roots to spread, punch holes in the sides or bottom of each peat pot, or simply remove the bottom before planting. Plant in a hole slightly larger than the pot so that the main stem is at least 2 inches deeper in the soil than it was originally. Set leggy, tall (over 10 inches) plants even deeper, or bury the stems in a sloping position, leaving only the top 5 to 6 inches above the ground. Press the soil firmly around each plant.

Before setting out plants grown in plastic, clay or paper pots, remove the pots without disturbing the roots. To remove plants from flats, use a trowel, and take care to leave as much soil as possible attached to the roots of each plant. Although bare-rooted tomato plants pulled from flats can withstand transplanting, plants with intact or undisturbed root systems grow more rapidly after setting and may produce fruits earlier.

Dry soil and hot weather are unfavorable for planting tomatoes. Do not let plants wilt during the process. If weather is hot or sunny, it is best to plant in late afternoon or evening.

— **Growing Garden Tomatoes**

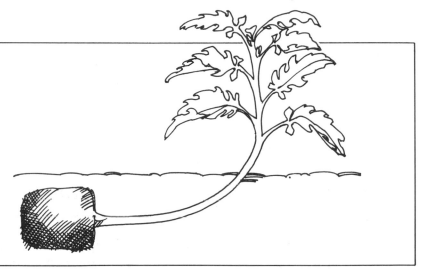

Planting the stem and root ball horizontally a few inches underground accomplishes two aims: it increases the root-growing capacity of the plant, which roots easily from its stem; and it ensures that the young plant will begin its outdoor growth in the warmest topsoil. Water top, stem and root ball after planting.

Ian S.R. Grainge

THE ACCELERATED WESTERNER

Usually, the outdoor Coast crop begins to ripen toward the end of August, with the main volume of fruit being harvested through September and early October. Unfortunately, after mid-September, quality and flavor deteriorate, and a large part of the crop may be affected by cracking skin, blight and rot.

Observations made over a number of years indicate that certain early varieties, if carefully grown, can have a good percentage of their fruit ripen during August and September when quality and flavor are at their best. Therefore, it is imperative to start with large, healthy plants of the recommended early varieties and to utilize all known techniques to accelerate growth and ripening.

A deep, silt loam on a slope facing south to southeast is the ideal location for an early harvest. Good crops can be grown on silty clay and other types of bottom land but usually will not be as early. In muck areas, plants are frequently over-vegetative and are more subject to blight and damage from frost in spring and fall. Plants grown on the south and even the west side of buildings, banks or board fences benefit from reflected heat.

Most Coast soils require an application of lime for best results. Soil may be tested to determine the amount of lime required. From 5 to 15 pounds per 100 square feet may be necessary. The lime should be incorporated into the soil at least two weeks before the plants are set.

A top dressing of manure should be applied in early spring. Alternatively, a green-manure cover crop may be grown the previous year and ploughed into the soil. Manures vary as to nutrient content and amount of straw. An application of 50 pounds per 100 square feet of cow manure, or half of this amount of chicken manure, will be beneficial.

— **Tomatoes in the Home Garden**

TENDER TOMATOES

Hardy crops are not only more frost-resistant but are also better able to grow in cool weather than are tender vegetables. The base temperature is that at which a crop ceases growing; for plants in general, the base temperature is averaged at 42 degrees F, but, more specifically, for spinach, it is 36 degrees, for lettuce 40 degrees, for peas 42 degrees, for corn and beans 50 degrees and for tomatoes and pumpkins 55.4 degrees. Not only do crops cease growing when the weather becomes cool, internal damage gradually progresses. Researchers at the University of California at Davis exposed eight-day-old tomato seedlings to 42-degree temperatures for various durations. When chilled for just two hours, "only slightly noticeable ultrastructural changes" took place, but deterioration became more severe as the duration of exposure increased. In another experiment, all five-day-old tomato seedlings, however well hardened, were killed by a seven-day exposure to a temperature of 34 degrees.

Why some plants are frost-hardy and others are not is still a matter for research, but the search has so far raised partial answers as well as some fascinating questions. Once, scientists postulated that, like animals, trees possessed their own "vital heat." How else could they survive the winter so well, while other plants shrivelled and died?

Trees do, in fact, freeze in the winter, but they are usually not harmed, although the same species that can survive laboratory freezing in liquid nitrogen at minus 32 degrees F in winter can often be felled by a temperature a few degrees below freezing in midsummer. The process, still not fully understood, by which plants prepare for winter's icy weather, is called acclimation, or hardening, and is triggered by dropping temperatures as well as changes in day length.

In the garden, the hardening process takes place, although few plants there will become as frost-resistant as native trees. Nevertheless, even tender plants do undergo some hardening. In 1967, two scientists showed that exposing five-day-old tomato seedlings grown at 77 degrees F to a conditioning temperature of 54.5 degrees for as little as three hours provided some protection from a subsequent exposure to 34 degrees. Clearly, garden plants are best able to endure a light frost that follows a period of increasingly cool weather, the normal autumn pattern. This is not only true because of the plants' inherent physical properties in fall but also because the gardener is less likely to have applied fertilizer late in the season. Such a procedure, which pro-

THE CHILLY OUTDOORS

In our Northern, temperate climate, tomatoes are not usually successful if seeded outdoors, because the seeds of most cultivars do not germinate satisfactorily in cold soil: at 50 degrees F, tomato seeds sprout in 25 to 30 days, compared with 4 to 5 days at 85 degrees. In most northern parts of the country, only early and mid-season varieties started from plants set out in the garden after danger of frost is past will ripen to a satisfactory crop.
— **Growing Garden Tomatoes**

duces tender, unacclimated growth, is an invitation to frost damage.

— JB

THE MANITOBA METHOD

Set out tomato plants after spring frosts are over. That is about June 10 in most localities but earlier in milder areas. If you cover the plants with paper protectors, you can transplant the tomatoes somewhat sooner, about May 25. Before using the protectors, ventilate them by cutting an opening three centimeters [one inch] in diameter in the peak. Enlarge the opening when the temperature goes above 24 degrees C [75 degrees F]. When frost threatens, place a second protector over the first one. Do not let the plants become overcrowded and deformed in the protectors. A deformed plant seldom produces good tomatoes. Allow the plants to grow out of the protectors freely, and finally, press the paper around the base of the plants where it will keep weeds down and conserve soil moisture.

At the research station at Morden, a system of growing tomato transplants was devised that promotes earlier fruiting and larger yields than the usual method. Plant protectors are an essential part of the system. Sow the seeds indoors on April 15, and set the transplants out in the garden on May 15. The weather may be cool. Therefore, shield the plants until they are planted, and then quickly cover them with paper protectors.

— Agriculture Canada Publication 1033
Growing Vegetables in the Prairie Garden

EDMONTON BUMPER CROPS

On a small city lot, we find it difficult to find enough warm spaces for tomatoes to enable us to rotate the all-important tomato crop to a new position every year, a practice recommended for the prevention of diseases and soil exhaustion. Nevertheless, even in Edmonton where summers are cool, we have managed to increase our tomato space by growing them in spots that are shaded for part of the day. For instance, we have had remarkable success growing tomatoes against the stucco wall of our house, which gets very hot during the day and radiates that heat through the night. Even when the overnight temperature dipped slightly below freezing, we did not need to cover the plants.

We have also had a bumper crop of tomatoes by planting them on the north side of a huge rock. The tomatoes were bordered on the west by a low hedge and were situated between the boulder and an as-

Harrowsmith Subscriptions: If card is missing, send $14.97 for a one-year subscription (six bimonthly issues) to HARROWSMITH, The Creamery, Charlotte, Vermont 05445.

YES. Please send my FREE COPY of *The Harrowsmith Tomato Handbook*, enter my risk-free subscription to HARROWSMITH and bill me at the special rate of $14.97 — six big bimonthly issues at a savings of 15 percent over the regular cover price.

SEND NO MONEY NOW

RISK-FREE GUARANTEE: If you are ever dissatisfied with HARROWSMITH, you may cancel for a full, prompt and courteous refund on all unmailed issues.

5012

BUSINESS REPLY MAIL

FIRST CLASS PERMIT NO. 5, CHARLOTTE, VT

POSTAGE WILL BE PAID BY ADDRESSEE

Harrowsmith

THE CREAMERY
CHARLOTTE, VERMONT 05445-9990

Cloches or row covers such as this one enhance the sun's heat around young tomatoes, speeding their growth in cool spring weather.

phalt driveway. The boulder and driveway and hedge trapped the heat from the sun so that the plants flourished even though they had full sun for only part of the day.

In the open garden, we ensured ourselves a good supply of tomatoes by making a simple hot-bed arrangement. First, we dug a hole a foot deep and three feet across. We dug chicken manure into the bottom of the hole and covered it with soil, leaving an eight-inch depression into which we poured water when necessary for irrigation. We then surrounded the area with sturdy stakes and tomato fence (not chicken wire, but larger-mesh fencing) and put the plants *outside* the fence. We regularly put kitchen compost inside the wire enclosure and covered this with soil each time. While air temperatures were still cool, the heat from the hot bed made melon seeds in the compost sprout and flourish before the tomato plants took off and shaded them.

— *E. Lozowski*
Edmonton, Alberta

TOMATO CAGES AND TOWERS

Tomato towers are square or cylindrical cages that force tomato plants to grow up rather than spread out. Towers permit the gardener to place plants closer together and harvest more fruit per square foot of garden space. Tomato plants grown in towers generally suffer less from disease and insect problems than plants allowed to sprawl on the ground. Only when persistently strong drying winds prevail do tomatoes grow better if allowed to sprawl.

The most common mistake in designing tomato towers is to make them too small. For the vigorous main-crop indeterminate tomato hybrids, towers should be 5 to 6 feet tall and 2½ feet across. The temptation to save money by making small, lightweight towers is also strong. Do not waste your money. Invest in large mesh, galvanized fence or the sturdy iron mesh used to reinforce concrete. Form it into a cylinder by bending it around a barrel. These big, rigid cylinders look as steady as the Rock of Gibraltar when you stand them in place, but they need one or two stakes that will keep them from toppling over in wind or rainstorms, especially when the plants are loaded with fruit.

Anyone reasonably skilled as a woodworker can make an excellent wooden tower from 1x2s. These need crossbars every foot vertically so that the tomato branches can be kept tucked inside. Design the cages so that the four verticals at the corners are pointed and can be buried a foot deep into the ground. Paint the entire structure with copper naphthanate for rot-proofing.

The ready-made cylindrical cages of heavy, galvanized wire that can be purchased in garden and department stores are usually large enough for small plants only. Chicken-wire cages are even less versatile, as the wire is not sufficiently strong and does not have large enough holes to enable the gardener to pick fruit through the sides of the towers.

— *National Garden Bureau*

A CAPITAL APPROACH

My selection of suitable seeds and the placing of my seed orders are only the first steps that enable me to harvest fruit all season. My cultural practices, also the result of experimentation, are equally important. First, I start the seeds of all my early tomatoes indoors during the first week of March. I place damp, sterile starting medium (available in any hardware or garden shop) in the perforated cells of an egg carton, two or three seeds per cup, one-quarter inch deep. I then tie a clear plastic bag around the carton and keep it quite warm, 75 to 90 degrees F. Tomato seeds will sprout in five or six days under these conditions but may take three weeks at 64 degrees. I remove the plastic bag as soon as the plants have emerged and then thin them to one seedling per cell.

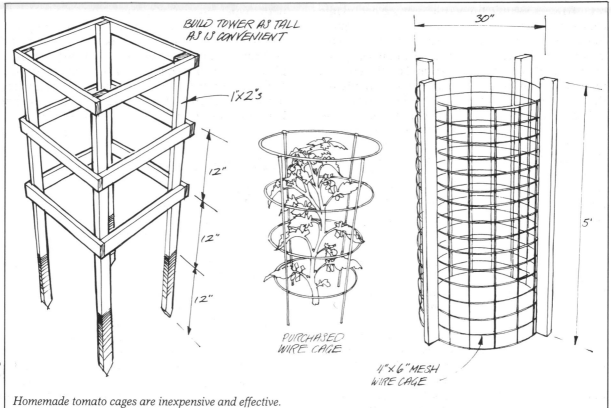

BUILD TOWER AS TALL
AS IS CONVENIENT

1"x2"s

12"

12"

12"

PURCHASED
WIRE CAGE

30"

5'

4"x6" MESH
WIRE CAGE

Ian S.R. Grainge

Homemade tomato cages are inexpensive and effective.

I use fluorescent fixtures and common cool-white bulbs as grow lights, keeping the tops of the plants just two inches below the lights. The intensity of the light decreases at a rate proportional to the square of the distance, so plants kept four inches away receive only one-quarter the light they do at two inches. Water sparingly, but do not let the plants wilt, and remove them from the egg cartons when they are two or three weeks old; this is very important to prevent root binding and stunting.

I place each of these young seedlings, complete with root ball, in a large paper or Styrofoam cup (its base perforated) filled with sterile potting mix. Now, however, the plants require fertilizer if they are not to turn yellow and weaken. I have found that a complete organic fertilizer is by far the best. It supplies all the necessary nutrients but does not burn or overstimulate the plant as synthetic fertilizers can. Water sparingly but regularly, always including the diluted organic fertilizer.

About six weeks later, the plants need transplanting again, as it is imperative that they not become rootbound and thus suffer a setback. Use a pair of scissors or a sharp knife to cut the cups away from the soil without disturbing the roots that hold the soil intact. For this final transplanting, I use a mixture of half garden soil and half peat moss in medium-sized plastic bags. The bags of soil are per-

National Garden Bureau

forated at the base and placed inside, supporting fiber pots that can be used year after year.

In these bags, the plants tend to become quite large, so two weeks later, I move them from beneath the fluorescents and set them in a small removable greenhouse that fronts my south-facing patio doors. Here, they grow and set fruit until about May 20. I place a small stake in each pot and tie the plant to it. If any leaves start to show signs of yellowing (the older ones are always the first to fade), I add extra fertilizer to the water. Despite advice to the contrary, I have found that flowering plants do not necessarily make poor transplants. The size of the pot used before transplanting and the growing conditions after planting are much more important than the age of the plant.

My early plants are usually set into a raised bed against the southeast wall of our house. This provides protection from cold northerly winds, an essential requirement if the many blossoms and fruits are to continue to develop at an optimal rate. Gardeners who do not have a protected, sunny location for large transplants should surround each plant with a wire tomato cage that has been wrapped with clear plastic. Leave the top open, and provide a small vent at the bottom of the south-facing side for ventilation on warm days.

Dig a large hole for each plant, setting it about as deep as its old level. Because my plants are very large and well developed, they do not require a planting deep enough to cover the stems, a procedure often recommended with tomato transplants. In fact, I do not like to plant the root ball too deep because the deeper soil can be cold and wet, even in early summer, slowing tomato growth. Gardeners not using raised beds should hill or mound the earth before planting their tomatoes so that the soil will drain more quickly and the sun will warm the earth faster, helping to hasten fruit maturity. Bone meal, which is high in phosphorus, also reduces the time to maturity. I always place about a cup around each root ball at planting time. As well, I give each transplant a drink of lukewarm water that contains fish fertilizer.

If they show signs of yellowing, I often give my tomatoes another feeding of fish fertilizer two or three weeks after transplanting. However, I do not use any nitrogen after this because while it may encourage leafy green growth, it also tends to retard fruit set and ripening. Too much nitrogen also promotes blossom drop and reduces the sugar level in the fruit, lessening flavor.

If possible, tomatoes should be planted about a foot and a half apart in a single line to allow sunshine to reach all parts of each plant. Place a four-foot-tall stake beside each plant. I use discarded hockey sticks sharpened at one end with a hole drilled in the other. A cord is run through these holes, connecting the line of stakes, to provide extra support when I later tie the plants to the stakes.

— *George Bushell*

STAKES AND OLD STOCKINGS

Most gardeners seem to prefer staked tomatoes rather than free-standing varieties, as they grow in a smaller area and are more suitable where space is limited. Staked plants are easier to cultivate and harvest, and the fruits are cleaner and free of ground roots. However, staked tomatoes tend to suffer greater losses of fruit from blossom-end rot, sunburn and cracking, and they require more hand labor for proper training.

Staking and pruning to a single stem is the most common training method. Preferably at the time of transplanting, place a stick, broom handle or wooden stake (1″ x 1″ x 5′) several inches from the plant, and push it deep into the soil. As the plant grows, use soft twine, rag or old stocking to tie the main stem to the stake but not tightly against it.

— **Growing Garden Tomatoes**

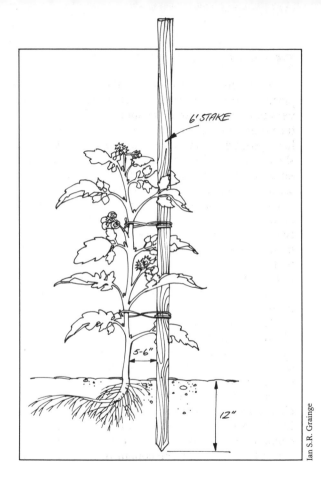

Ian S.R. Grainge

PLASTIC MULCH

By mulching both row and hill crops with clear plastic, Garit Tenpas and Dale Schlough of the University of Wisconsin have successfully grown watermelons on the chilly shores of Lake Superior and have produced 10 years of experimental data which show that muskmelons, tomatoes, corn, cucumbers and squash can all be grown in areas formerly considered inhospitable to warm-weather crops.

The Wisconsin research shows that the ripening date of some vegetables can be hastened by up to two weeks, while yields also increase substantially in most cases, dramatically in others. Early tomatoes, for example, showed a 119 percent increase in total harvest when grown with clear plastic.

In effect creating a ground-hugging mini-greenhouse atmosphere, the clear plastic works to raise soil temperature, thus improving the immediate environment of seeds and tender young plants at the beginning of the growing season. Research has shown that soil under the clear plastic is often 20 degrees warmer than uncovered ground nearby.

Plastic mulch, of course, is hardly a new idea. The clear plastic is an obvious spin-off from the use of black plastic mulch, which has gained general acceptance as a weed retardant and moisture retainer.

But the results in Wisconsin indicate that clear plastic has definite advantages over the widely used black material. Tenpas and Schlough say that black plastic absorbs heat but that soil temperature increases only at the soil surface, just below the sheet of plastic.

If an airspace develops between the plastic and the earth, the soil is barely heated at all. Even if it is put down properly, cool winds blowing over the surface quickly dissipate the heat that has accumulated.

Initial trials at the Ashland experiment station convinced the researchers that soil under clear film not only warmed more quickly but that it retained its warmth through cool nights.

The number of early tomatoes jumped by 76 percent, with the average weight per tomato up 23 percent. Late tomatoes showed production increases with clear plastic, but the improvements were not as spectacular as with the early varieties.

Because of the warmth and moisture trapped in the plant's root zone, growth is stimulated, resulting in the earlier ripening and better yields observed. The mulch has been most effective in heavy wet soils.

Excessive weed growth beneath clear plastic has been the drawback most frequently cited by those who feel that it is impractical. Yet Schlough says, "We have used clear plastic for 10 years and have

cause of the excessive heat and moisture retained by the plastic.

"Even with weeds present beneath the plastic, we have recorded 200 to 400 percent increases in the yields of some crops."

Schlough says that the plastic may balloon out with weeds, but it can be removed after July 1, or once the full warmth of the summer is assured. The greatest benefit from the film has already been achieved by the time weeds become a problem, he says.

The major drawbacks for home gardeners are aesthetics and cost. Plastic is not the most natural of substances, but for those in northern areas, the alternatives will be to buy food grown on southern California megafarms or to build a greenhouse.

Other drawbacks include the extra time required to lay the plastic and the increased possibility of frost damage early and late in the growing season. Schlough explains that plastic retains heat in the earth, and the warmth that normally radiates from unmulched soil and can save plants from being damaged by frost is prevented from escaping.

Cool-weather crops that should not need plastic mulch in most climates are peas, beans, carrots and spinach. Subarctic gardeners, however, may find clear plastic a boon to even these vegetables.

Agriculture Canada has reported 16 degree F in-

encountered no serious weed problems. Yes, weeds can grow beneath the plastic in a tangled, green mass, but if the plastic is anchored tightly to the earth, the weeds become spindly and unhealthy be-

creases of soil temperature with clear plastic, which can also be stretched over small frames to cover the plant foliage as well.

Cornell University has tried, with success, creating a trench for such crops as corn and stretching clear plastic over the trench to give such vegetables a running jump on the growing season (they find the film must be removed when the weeds start to become a problem).

Schlough and Tenpas are now directing their experiments with clear plastic toward cold-climate crops such as the *Brassicas*. "We have had ripe cauliflower and broccoli by July 1," Schlough told us, "but we found that forcing the plants produces very loose heads."

My own abiding goal is to ripen a tomato by July 1. Using clear plastic mulch and some new *Sub-Arctic* varieties I have recently come across, I am convinced that my ambition may not be as outlandish as it seems.

— *Jeffrey C. Hautala*

Scientific research has proved that a plastic mulch can significantly warm the soil, speeding tomato maturation in a cool climate.

The Formative Weeks

Tender, Loving Cultivation

What wondrous life is this I lead£
Ripe apples drop about my head;
The nectarine and curious peach
Into my hands themselves do reach;
Stumbling on melons as I pass
Insnared with flowers, I fall on grass.

Andrew Marvell's celebration of the summer garden makes no mention of the sweet fragrance and flavor of the first ripe tomato, a lapse that is understandable, for in 17th-century England, the tomato was still considered a curiosity of possibly dangerous intent. Nor are considerably less poetic aspects of the warmest season described: weeds, drought, insects and even plant diseases. Still, the gardener who expends a little extra effort near the finish line may be inspired soon enough to compose his own ode. As Thomas Whiteside wrote in an article on tomatoes in *The New Yorker* in 1977, "When I take a tomato from the vine on a fine day in August or early September – the height of the growing season in the northeast – and cut it open, I feel as though I could taste sunshine itself in the plump, tender fruit."

– JB

A crop of tomatoes lovingly grown by Raffaele Cristofaro, using Old World organic techniques that serve him well in a cold climate.

THE TOMATO WARD

Hundreds of generations removed from their tough little South American ancestors, today's tomato plants with their huge, thin-skinned fruits have become easy marks for a host of wilts, blights, rots, spots and mosaics. North American varieties of *Lycopersicon esculentum* may be attacked by one or more of some 50 common afflictions, including such richly named horrors as blackheart, tobacco etch, catface, buckeye rot and ghost spot. Although many gardeners go years without a serious tomato problem, there are seasons when things seem to take a page out of Lewis Carroll and become "curiouser and curiouser."

The orthodox approach, still widely touted by radio columnists and mainstream garden writers, is to spray and dust the tomato patch regularly, whether it needs it or not. To these growers, tomato culture would not be complete without face mask, rubber gloves and sacks of Malathion, Maneb and Carbaryl. This, of course, is the California system in miniature; there, many growers routinely sterilize their fields, lay a plastic mulch and, at regularly scheduled intervals, dispense fungicides and pesticides until the fruit is picked, still green enough and hard enough to withstand anything short of a direct hit of a forklift tire. Much of this frenetic and anti-septic activity is done for the benefit of the supermarket shopper; beauty in the celluloid tomato package is as deep as a clear, pale pink skin.

Fortunately, most gardeners are much more tolerant of imperfections. (As the old saying goes, "Every mother thinks her own geese are swans.") The organic gardener, especially, may be willing to accept the occasional blemish in return for a residue-free harvest of fully ripe, deep red tomatoes that have completed their flavor development. (Box-ripened commercial fruits suffer from containing too much starch, too little natural sugar and appreciably lower levels of vitamin C, or ascorbic acid.)

Flavor, in fact, is a factor that seldom enters into present-day commercial tomato production, in

OPEN CENTERS

Bush or determinate varieties are usually not pruned, but if growth is very vigorous, thin the center of the plant. This will open up the plant and hasten ripening.

— **Tomatoes in the Home Garden**

which sheer quantity and external appearance count for all. Crowding of plants, lack of crop rotation and the culture of a single variety – all conditions that encourage disease and serious pest damage – are almost endemic in commercial tomato farming but are easily avoided in the home garden.

Disease management – minimizing the possibility of a disease starting, or modifying its effects should it get a foothold – rather than ironclad control, the complete eradication of disease, should be the goal. It is now generally recognized that pesticide and fungicide use tends to lead to an ever-increasing need for pesticides and fungicides, and the backyard gardener is wise to avoid or interrupt such a cycle.

Fortunately for those of us who savor a truly garden-fresh, juicy tomato, the factors that encourage high productivity and good flavor are intertwined with the nonchemical practices of disease management.

The organic garden health-care plan for tomatoes is based on the proverbial "ounce of prevention" – from seed choice to tomato harvest and fall cleanup. The first step, of course, is to recognize the pestilence that has visited one's tomato rows, and then begin a course of action to moderate its effects or evade its path next year.

Having bred the natural broad-spectrum disease resistance out of the tomato, man is now industriously putting it back, malady by malady. "Resistance," as a descriptive term in the seed catalogues, means virtual immunity to a particular disease, and it is a factor well worth noting in selecting seed or buying transplants. The inbred resistance is usually created by crossing domesticated tomato varieties with wild relatives that have inborn resistance. The native South American *Lycopersicon hirsutum*, for instance, has a natural pest resistance and may lead to the development of future varieties that pests will shun. Such resistance can also be achieved, painstakingly, by grafting. Some varieties of nightshade are resistant to soil-borne wilt diseases; if a tomato is grafted onto such a rootstock, it will inherit the resistance. (Grafting research hit a temporary cul-de-sac when a tomato was grafted onto a nematode-resistant jimson weed root. The nematodes wisely steered clear of the plant, whose natural toxins suffused the roots, the vine and the fruit, making it inedible.) Genetic changes induced by certain chemicals or by radiation may also confer disease resistance upon a new tomato variety.

Plants that are resistant to verticillium wilt, one of the most common and destructive fungus diseases, are marked with the letter V or VR after the variety name. The letter F indicates resistance to fusarium wilt, and N is added if the plant is resistant to attack by nematodes. For example, Stokes Seeds' catalogue describes *Ultra Boy VFN* thus: *"Ultra Boy's* multi-tolerance to verticillium, fusarium and nematodes provides market gardeners and home gardeners with a good protection from troublesome wilts and blights. This disease tolerance lengthens the growing season and enables growers to pick amazing yields per plant – if properly cared for and fertilized."* (VF is sufficiently important that some commercial varieties dispense entirely with more descriptive names. The most popular variety among commercial growers in California is the mundanely labelled *VF 145*.)

Resistance to fruit cracking is often mentioned in the variety description. *Burpee's VF Hybrid*, while not resistant to nematodes, is described as having "amazing crack resistance."

Other varieties are "tolerant" to certain diseases – that is, they may be affected in an epidemic but will probably not be killed. Tolerance is usually mentioned in the variety description. For instance, *Veemore* tomatoes, though they do not receive the VF label, are described by one seedsman as "tolerant to both verticillium and fusarium." Tolerance is ample protection in most home-garden situations.

It is important to note that disease resistance is no guarantee of good flavor, and many organic gardeners decide to risk a disease outbreak in favor of a well-loved variety that is, as far as catalogue descriptions indicate, utterly defenseless. Many gardeners save, and swear by, seed of a favored nonhybrid tomato whose offspring, unprotected by genetic armor, produce bountiful harvests every year. On the other hand, the variety *Floramerica VFN*, an All-America award winner, may be resistant to VFN and tolerant to another dozen or so diseases, but its flavor has been found to be mediocre by some gardeners. Furthermore, VFN varieties may be just as vulnerable to unlisted ailments as are any other varieties. The *Beefeater Hybrid VFN* plants, grown by one gardener of our acquaintance, were initially set back by blossom-end rot and blackheart but eventually produced large, delicious fruit. A gardener will be wise to grow more than one variety each year, if possible, to provide a measure of "health insurance" and to vary the harvest.

GOOD EARTH

Although the tomato plant is widely adapted to diverse environments, it thrives best under full sunlight and in a fertile, well-drained soil high in organic matter. Tomatoes grown in shade conditions have little chance of maturing fruit, while those grown in depleted soil will be scraggly and unproductive; in both cases, the plants are decidedly more vulnerable to disease and pest damage than healthy vines.

Old hands at tomato culture are aware of the value

of rich soil, and most have fallen into a pattern of adding fresh manure to the space that will host their tomatoes the following spring or of working well-rotted manure or good compost into the soil two or three weeks before setting out the new transplants. Tomatoes are among the heaviest of garden feeders, and fertile soil not only helps minimize disease problems but prevents disorders related to deficiencies in soil nutrients. (A boron shortage, for instance, will produce misshapen tomatoes with scabby or corky patches on the skin.) In addition to animal manures and compost, tomato grounds benefit from the tilling in of wood ashes, which supply potassium and bone meal, rich in phosphorus.

Tomatoes in most soils respond well to a booster dose of manure "tea" or other highly soluble fertilizer early in the growing season. By the time the first fruits are the size of golf balls, the gardener should pour a bucket of manure tea or fertilizer solution around each plant. Manure tea is an unappetizing brew made by steeping healthy handfuls of fresh or rotten manure overnight in a pailful of water. The resulting liquid is infused with nutrients, which easily soak in around the tomato roots to encourage adequate plant growth and good sizing of the fruit. Fish fertilizer emulsions and blood meal, which is highly soluble, will achieve the same results.

Too much fertilization, however, can encourage

WINTER CUTTINGS

One summer, I read that you could get tomato plants from cuttings. I tried it, and it was more successful than I could have imagined. In late August, I took four sturdy cuttings (no flowers on them) from healthy tomato plants growing in my garden. I potted these in sterilized potting soil in 8-inch and 10-inch flower pots with good drainage. I watered them well and allowed them to drain.

I potted these in sterilized potting soil in 8-inch and 10-inch flower pots with good drainage. I watered them well and allowed them to drain.

I covered these pots with large, clear plastic bags held away from the plant with wire shaped into a dome and held around the pot with elastic bands. At first, I left the pots outside on the patio and, as the plants took root, opened the plastic covers bit by bit. Later, I brought the pots indoors and put them in my sunniest window. I watered them regularly. When flowers developed, I shook the plants gently to pollinate. Best of all, we enjoyed delicious tomatoes — the first red ones came in mid-November, and we had our own tomatoes at Christmas.

— *E. Lozowski*

over-exuberant foliage growth to the detriment of fruit development. If overfed by fresh manure or by too heavy application of any nitrogen-rich fertilizer, blossoms may drop, rendering the vine useless but for its beauty as a green plant.

LOCATIONS

In setting tomato plants out, the rule of thumb is to leave three feet between rows and three feet between individual vines. Staked tomatoes—the so-called indeterminate varieties—may be planted somewhat closer as may vines that will be trained up a wall or trellis.

To minimize the possibility of the spread of disease from one vegetable species to another, do not plant the tomato's garden relatives – eggplant, peppers, potatoes or tobacco – near their red-fruited kin. Cucumbers and melons can also host tomato diseases. Leaf crops, onions, root crops, herbs or *Brassicas* like cabbage, Brussels sprouts and broccoli are better bed mates for tomatoes. Nearby basil plants are rumored to enhance tomato flavor, while marigolds, which can help ward off nematodes, are a particularly good companion crop. A chemical component of asparagus will also help prevent nematode infestation, and while it is hardly practical to plant tomatoes in the perennial asparagus bed, the organic gardener can take advantage of this valua-

PRUNING TECHNIQUES

Prune tomatoes by snapping off small side shoots as they develop where the leaf stems join the main stem. Flower clusters arise directly from the stem. To prevent development of fruits that will not mature within the harvest season, remove all flower clusters forming after the end of July, or less than 60 days before the anticipated date of first frost in the fall. This conserves food manufactured by the plant for fruits already set. The common practice of removing the tip of the plant when it reaches the top of the stake may not be of any advantage, since tip removal may limit the plant's leaf area.

— **Growing Garden Tomatoes**

ble quality by pouring the water from cooked asparagus around his tomato seedlings.

Every year, the tomato plants should be set in a different spot in the garden so that any one spot is used no more frequently than once every three years. This helps soil fertility – different crops util-

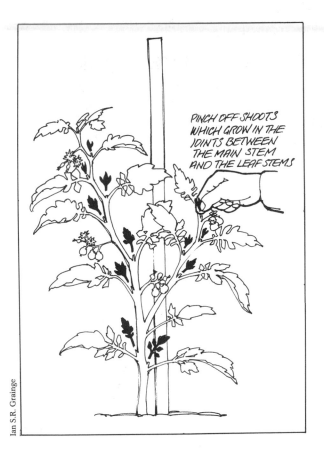

PINCH OFF SHOOTS WHICH GROW IN THE JOINTS BETWEEN THE MAIN STEM AND THE LEAF STEMS

Ian S.R. Grainge

ize, or even add, different nutrients — and also helps discourage diseases that live in decaying bits of tomato vegetation or in the soil where tomatoes were grown. In addition, tomatoes should not be planted where a botanical relative was sown the previous year.

One key to disease control is the elimination of any plant material that may harbor pathogenic organisms over the winter. Any diseased tomatoes or vines that appear should be collected and disposed of well away from the garden — not added to the compost pile or simply turned back into the soil. If a viral, fungal or bacterial outbreak occurs in an entire patch, all vegetation should be properly disposed of outside the confines of the garden once the season or the plants are finished. (The same holds true for diseased potatoes and potato vines, which can serve as a wintering ground for serious problems.)

Part and parcel of any disease control or prevention program is the ability to recognize the different common tomato maladies, after which one can work to thwart them or at least lessen their ravages. The following problems are those most frequently encountered by gardeners in the northern United States.

FUNGAL DISEASES

Fungal diseases include many different "blights" and "wilts" and are caused by microscopic parasitic plants that live on plants and on dead organic matter. Encouraged by damp, warm, overcrowded conditions, they produce spores that blow or are brushed or washed from plant to plant. Such spores often overwinter in rotting vegetation in the soil and erupt again when conditions are favorable. Anything that encourages good air circulation and good soil drainage and minimizes the handling of damp plants will help discourage fungal diseases.

Damping Off is caused by various fungi that live in the soil. It attacks young seedlings before or after they emerge from the soil, until they are about two weeks old. The affected stem shrivels and darkens at the soil line so that the young plant topples and dies.

When starting seeds indoors, you should sterilize garden soil before planting. As a further precaution, peat moss, which is slightly acidic and inhibits the fungus, can be mixed into the soil or sprinkled over it. Sterilized potting soil or components such as peat moss, vermiculite or perlite need not be sterilized. Water the seed medium and seedlings only when almost dry. Excessive dampness favors fungal growth — hence the name "damping off."

Early Blight is also known as "target spot" because of the circular dark brown or black spots of concentric rings that appear on affected leaves, which eventually die and drop off. When it attacks the stem with a black lesion, the disease is often called "collar rot." Although infection of the fruit itself is rare in the home garden, partial defoliation of the plant will nevertheless lower fruit size and quality.

Like damping off, early blight often attacks young seedlings. It, too, can be discouraged with a sterilized planting medium and by giving seedlings ample space in well-drained flats. If seedlings become infected before transplanting, discard them.

Septoria Leaf Spot flourishes in times of heavy rain and warm weather, producing small, circular, gray- to tan-colored spots on the lower leaves, stems and petioles (the small stems that support each leaf). In the center of these spots, small black "pimples," the fruiting bodies of the fungus, may be seen with a hand lens or sometimes by the naked eye. Millions of spores produced in these pimples are splashed about by rain and irrigation and give rise to new infections in a few days. Infected leaves dry out and die from the base of the plant upward. Although the fruits are rarely affected, fruit size and quality are lowered as the plant weakens from leaf loss, and the remaining fruit may be exposed to sunscald.

Resistance to verticillium wilt, fusarium wilt and nematodes is indicated by the initials V, F and N after a tomato name.

This fungus can overwinter on weeds or the remains of tomato plants. Be sure to plough in all remaining (healthy) tomato vegetation when the harvest is complete, or remove it to the compost pile. The remains of affected plants should be discarded away from the garden.

Late Blight erupts during the showery, cloudy days of late summer. It is not usually seen until a heavy foliage has developed and harvest has commenced. Although it is more commonly a disease of potatoes, late blight can be passed from infected potatoes to tomato plants (or vice versa) and will infest tomatoes severely. Greenish black spots appear on the oldest leaves, enlarging rapidly. (The rapid spread of crop diseases such as this led to the term "wild fire.") Bluish gray fungus may appear under the leaves, virtually all of which will die. Infected, rotten fruits exude a musty, disagreeable odor.

Destroy affected tomato or potato plants and all tubers. Potatoes and tomatoes should not be interplanted in the garden. If late blight has been a problem, choose a blight-resistant variety like *New Yorker* standard-sized tomatoes or *Nova* paste tomatoes the following year.

Anthracnose is a disease of ripe, red fruit. Spores of the fungus are spread by rain to green fruits where infection occurs, although it is not evident until the fruit ripens. Small, slightly sunken circular spots appear and grow up to one-half inch in diameter, often merging to cover most of the fruit, particularly the lower side. The skin over these spots may crack, allowing other fungi to grow. Serious wastage results because the gardener must cut away blemished areas before eating or canning fruit.

This fungus persists through the winter on infected plant refuse. Remove all such vegetation after harvest, and discard it away from the garden. Do not plant tomatoes or a relative in the affected spot in the garden for two or three years. Supporting the fruit above the ground will help prevent anthracnose infection.

Verticillium Wilt is one of the most destructive of garden fungi, with strains attacking potatoes, peppers, melons and some berries and fruits as well as tomatoes. The fungus is capable of surviving several years in soil debris, then entering the roots and invading the water-conducting system of the plant. It is first evident as the wilting of one or two leaflets of a single, lower leaf. Leaves wilt and die progressively from the base to the top of the plant, sometimes on one side of the plant only. The plant itself may not die but will produce small fruit.

Choose resistant or tolerant varieties if verticillium wilt has been a problem.

VIRAL DISEASES
Viral diseases, the "mosaics," are caused by organisms so minuscule that they can be seen only with
an electron microscope. Often transmitted from

WEED 'EM AND REAP

As soon as the soil can be properly worked after each rain or irrigation, it should be thoroughly hoed or cultivated to kill weeds that have sprouted and to leave the surface in a loose, friable condition to absorb later rainfall. The primary value of hoeing or cultivating is weed control. This cultivation should be shallow so as to avoid injuring the vegetable plant roots that lie near the surface.

In small gardens, weeds can be controlled with black polyethylene mulch supplemented by hand weeding, such as pulling, hoeing and wheel hoeing. Mulching vegetable crops with organic material also is a common practice in small gardens.

The best organic mulches are partially decomposed hay, straw or grass clippings. The mulch should be applied four to six inches deep when the plants are about six inches tall. Not only does mulch control weeds, it also conserves moisture, keeps the soil from packing and increases the humus necessary for vigorous plant growth.

– *United States Department of Agriculture*
Growing Vegetables in the Home Garden

host plants by insects like aphids or by the gardener himself, virus-caused diseases are best prevented by a conscientious program of cleanliness.

Tomato Mosaic, known commercially as **TMV**, and **Cucumber Mosaic** cause light to dark green mottling of the leaves – a mosaic effect. Leaflets are usually distorted, puckered and smaller than usual, sometimes assuming an indented fern shape. Plants will usually become pale green and spindly, and the harvest will be small and late.

Highly infectious, mosaics are transmitted by leaf pruning and plant handling and from such plants as petunias, snapdragons, peppers and tobacco. Do not grow tomatoes near these plants. It can also be present in smoking or chewing tobacco, so if the gardener uses tobacco, he should wash his hands thoroughly with soap and water before handling tomato plants. Cucumber mosaic is often transmitted by aphids, especially when cucumbers or melons and tomatoes are interplanted.

BACTERIAL DISEASES

Bacterial diseases are caused by single-celled organisms. Seldom a serious problem in the home garden, they may, however, present difficulties in a crowded, closed greenhouse environment (where virtually all types of diseases are likely to thrive).

In the greenhouse, use a sterilized medium for starting seedlings and for larger plants as well, if possible. Diseases like **Bacterial Canker, Bacterial Spot** and **Bacterial Speck** can be discouraged by disinfecting pruning tools frequently and washing one's hands often while working with tomato plants.

The first symptom of a bacterial disease is the wilting of leaflets. They become brown, dying from the margins toward the midribs. There may be a blackish speckling or spotting of fruit. Infected plants may die, or they may survive in a wilted condition, bearing little fruit. Such plants must be removed and destroyed as soon as disease symptoms are noted. Any plants that have come in contact with the diseased plant should be destroyed also.

NONPARASITIC DISEASES

Nonparasitic diseases erupt when environmental conditions are less than ideal. They are not spread to or from other plants but are temporary conditions that will pass when growing conditions improve.

Blossom-End Rot usually develops on the first fruits of a plant to ripen or on clusters of fruits formed during a prolonged hot, dry period. A hard, sunken, dark area appears on the blossom (lower) **85**

end of the fruit and spreads as the tomato ripens. The repulsive internal blackening, called **Blackheart**, is caused by the same conditions but may be present without the external symptoms appearing.

Blossom-end rot and blackheart may also be caused by a calcium deficiency in the soil. Calcium, which is required by rapidly growing plants, can be added to the soil in the form of finely ground limestone, gypsum or eggshells before the plants are set out in the garden. Deep watering every week during droughts will help discourage the disorder. Mulch young plants in spring. If blossom-end rot is noticed, pick all damaged fruits, and discard them, leaving the plant to put its strength into the healthy fruit.

Fruit Cracking is a response to radical changes in temperature and moisture, usually wet weather following hot, dry conditions. Concentric circular or radial, outward-pointing cracks develop at the stem end and may provide entrance for fungi and other diseases.

Little can be done to prevent fruit cracking of susceptible varieties, although a consistent watering program may help: cracking, like blossom-end rot, can be reduced by mulching plants. It may be necessary to pick affected fruits before they are entirely ripe, allowing them to ripen indoors so that cracks will not become infected. Choose crack-resistant varieties.

CAN DO REACTOR

When we left to go on holiday last April and my tomato plants in the garden were only about five inches tall, I reasoned that if I put a shelter board behind each one on the north side and a tall juice can close by on the east and west side, each plant would be in a slightly protected den should a mild frost occur. Of my 17 plants, I did eight this way, and they had advanced to double the size of the unprotected ones by the time we returned to Victoria two weeks later. So we left the cans there, and by the end of June, the protected plants were three times the size of the unprotected ones. This effect may be more noticeable here than it would be elsewhere in Canada, as we do not get high heat, but I believe that the tomato-enhancement effect must have been caused by the cans' conducting heat into the soil. I had left the bases on the cans and overturned them, burying each one about 1½ to 2 inches into the soil. A couple of plants protected with just two angled boards did not produce such a striking difference in growth.

— Stan Biram

Leather-End is characterized by bronzing and roughening of the skin at the stem end of the fruit. This affects only the appearance of the fruit and the texture of the affected skin. The disorder develops late in the season, when the weather is cloudy and the nights are cool. It also develops on cultivars with dark green shoulders, and can be prevented by using a fertilizer higher in potash. Gardeners who have persistent problems with leather-end can pick the fruit while it is still green and let it ripen indoors.

Tin-can shelters increased the growth of Stan Biram's crop.

Ian S.R. Grainge

Sunscald may occur whenever green or ripening fruits are exposed to the hot sun for several days. A yellowish white area of sunken tissue appears on the side of the fruit facing the sun. This may turn blistery and will flatten to a large, grayish white spot with a very thin paperlike surface. Fungus infections often occur on such spots.

Defoliation, whether caused by excessive pruning or attack by disease, encourages sunscald; plants may require shading with cloth. Verticillium-wilt-resistant varieties are also resistant to sunscald.

Walnut Wilt is an example of a negative sort of companion planting. Walnut tree roots secrete juglone, a toxin that kills tomato plants. Do not plant tomatoes within 40 or 50 feet of a walnut tree or on land from which a walnut tree has been removed within the last three years.

Catface is a distortion of the blossom end of the tomato. Occurring most commonly on first fruits, it often causes protuberances, scabs and scaly dark green scar tissue in folds. Affected fruits are edible once the scarred portion has been removed.

This temporary condition is caused by an abnormal development of the pistil of the tomato blossom and is aggravated by serious disturbances to growth, such as prolonged cool weather during blossoming.

Leaf Roll is common, temporary and not a cause for concern. The edges of the leaves roll upward and inward, overlapping in severe cases. However, the growth of the plant is not checked, and a normal harvest of fruit is produced. Leaf roll is genetically caused. It helps expose fruit to the sun and so hastens maturity.

Blossom Drop: If a tomato plant is under stress, blossoms may simply grow and fall off because fruit growth requires a great deal of plant energy. Conditions that cause blossom drop include extreme temperatures, either too hot or too cold, or sudden, drastic changes in temperature. It can also be caused by too little light (less than six hours daily), too much or too little water or overfertilization. Also, if blossoms are unfertilized, they will fall off, but this is a problem only in the greenhouse and can be solved by lightly shaking flowering plants or hand-pollinating flowers with an artist's brush.

Frost Damage occurs if fruit is frozen or exposed to frost. Exposed areas become dark and soft, appear water-soaked and will deteriorate rapidly. Cover plants when light frost is expected, and pick all fruit before a hard frost (temperatures under 30 degrees F). If fruit is damaged, use as soon as possible.

— *Harrowsmith Staff*

CUTTING COMMENTS

Generally the easiest of all plants to propagate from cuttings, or "slips," herbaceous or nonwoody plants often reward even the most negligent gardener with a healthy root system within weeks.

Tomatoes are good examples of nonwoody plants whose cuttings root easily. Any sucker that forms in a leaf axil or crotch throughout the summer can be snapped off at its base and buried two-thirds deep in the garden or in potting soil indoors. Kept wet until roots form in two or three weeks, they give the gardener a late harvest of the same type of fruit produced by the parent, whether open-pollinated or hybrid. As these suckers are usually removed as a matter of course in the pruning of staked plants, their production of added fruit is a bonus for good gardening. Suckers brought indoors in fall and rooted in plant pots can be used to overwinter a favorite hybrid variety, perhaps one whose seeds are expensive or difficult to obtain. In spring, again take cuttings from the plant, which will by then be tall and gangly. Root them in individual pots, and then treat them like any other vegetable transplant, hardening them off before planting them outdoors.

— *JB*

GARDENER, KNOW THY BUGS

Although there are some 80,000 species of insects in the world, the average garden will probably see only one or two a season that seriously threaten the harvest. Ecologically aware gardeners will deal with these outbreaks swiftly – plants can be set back very quickly by such insects as the Colorado potato beetle or Mexican bean beetle – but without blanketing an entire plot with pesticides.

By recognizing the insect and attacking it, and it alone, we can minimize harm to the beneficial insects that usually keep pests in check. Even the mildest of chemical insecticides – such as Sevin – recommended by the majority of gardening magazines, are death to honeybees and many insect predators.

The most sensible progression is this: (1) Pick the offenders by hand, if possible. Small numbers of most insects are easily controlled and can often be tolerated. A blast of water may even be enough to dislodge certain caterpillars or aphids that will perish once separated from their food source.

(2) Repellent sprays do work, most notably those heavy with garlic. Controlled experiments have verified the effectiveness of this English decoction:

Chop or blend three ounces of garlic, and let it soak in about two teaspoons of mineral oil for one day. Add one pint of water that contains one-quarter ounce of pure soap (not detergent). Stir or blend, and then strain through several layers of cheesecloth.

This may be diluted at about 1 part to 20 parts of fresh water and sprayed on the vegetables or flowers to be protected. Store in a glass or plastic container (the spray will react with metal).

(3) Turn to rotenone, pyrethrum or *Bacillus thuringiensis* (Bt) if necessary. All are derived from natural sources.

Rotenone, from various South American roots, can be used against many garden insects, and many growers use nothing else. Pyrethrum comes from the pyrethrum daisy and has better knock-down power but is harder on the beneficial insects.

Bt is a bacterial disease that stops most caterpillars (*Lepidoptera* larvae) from eating within 24 hours and then kills them. It comes in a powder (endospores) that is mixed with water and sprayed. Trade names are Dipel, Thuricide and Biotrol.

But before setting out to decimate the ranks of an insect that has suddenly appeared in your tomato patch, be sure to know your adversary. There are many more beneficial insects than the average gardener realizes, and they should be protected. Other bugs are more fearsome than destructive. The following guide shows some of the more common North American pests and beneficial insects.

TOBACCO HORNWORM (*Protoparce sexta*): It is likely that you will discover this huge caterpillar's handiwork before you find the actual insect. Evidence will include denuded branches on any of its solanaceous hosts (the nightshade group of tomatoes, peppers, eggplant and tobacco). Droppings approaching the size of mouse feces will be found under the plant.

The tobacco hornworm has seven diagonal stripes and a reddish horn at the rear, while its near relative the tomato hornworm has eight and its prong-like horn at the rear is green. Both attack the same plants. The adult form is the large grey-brown sphynx moth, also known as the hawk, or hummingbird, moth.

Control: Handpicking is usually enough to eradicate these impressive insects, as they often appear singly or in numbers of less than a dozen. Larger infestations may be cleaned out with the use of Bt.

COLORADO POTATO BEETLE (*Leptinotarsa decemilineata*): Many gardeners find this the worst of summer's pests and one that is well able to strip an entire crop of potatoes of its foliage or turn rows of tomato plants into barely visible stubs.

Curiously, the insect was almost unheard of until settlers brought the potato to North America. The Colorado potato beetle had lived in obscurity in the foothills of the Rocky Mountains, feeding mainly on sandbar weed, but found the potato to its liking and began moving eastward at a rate of 85 miles per year. It managed to reach even Europe with World War I supply ships, despite frantic efforts to stop it at the Atlantic.

Control: Small infestations may be curbed by handpicking, but many gardeners will turn to regular applications of rotenone in bad years.

CUTWORM (*Nephelodes emmedonia*) and others: One of the most insidious of common garden insects, the cutworm works only at night and may take down whole rows of tender seedlings in short order.

Some varieties work just below the surface of the soil, while others nip off the stalk just above the ground. Their adult form is a night-flying moth, while the pupal stage is a shelled case commonly seen when tilling or forking over garden soil.

Cutworms attack mainly cabbages, tomatoes and beans, but other crops are also vulnerable.

Control: The above-surface cutworms can be spotted easily at night with a flashlight and handpicked. Many gardeners put a handful of wood ash around new transplants, while others stick a toothpick in the soil immediately next to the stem. The cutworm, which encircles the stem to eat it, will find this ob-

TEMPERATE NIGHTS

Tomatoes have an optimum temperature range for fruit setting, with some varieties having a wider range than others. Especially during the early part of the growing season, the loss of tomato flowers can be attributed to too-low night temperatures while the flowers are open. With many tomato varieties, night temperatures below 58 to 60 degrees F will either injure the pollen grains or impair the fertilization process. Some varieties, including *Fireball, New Yorker, Starfire* and *Springset*, have more tolerance and will often set fruit when temperatures are dropping to 55 degrees or a little below. Tomatoes also may set fruit poorly when night temperatures remain above 73 to 75 degrees.

— *Suffolk County Agricultural Newsletter New York State, 1980*

struction and, it is hoped, move on.

NEMATODES, or eelworms, family Nematoda: These tiny, often microscopic, transparent, soil-dwelling roundworms infest practically every crop, including tomatoes, whose roots they may invade, causing the formation of knots that impede the uptake of water and nutrients so that plants stop growing and sometimes die. Fortunately, nematodes seldom pose a severe problem to tomatoes grown outdoors in the north.

Control: The initial **N** with a cultivar name indicates that a tomato has inbred nematode resistance. Soil sterilization kills the pests, and some *Tagetes* marigolds such as *Goldie* and *Tangerine* are able to rid soil of nematodes provided they are planted closely and allowed to grow for at least 90 days, a treatment that lasts about a year. Although the value of interplanting tomatoes and marigolds does not have scientific backing, it certainly can't hurt.

LADYBIRD BEETLE, family Coccinellidae: The adult ladybird beetle, or ladybug, is familiar to everyone, but little known is its important larval form.

Both adults and larvae have insatiable appetites for aphids, and they also form an important natural control of scale insects and mealy bugs.

There are numerous forms within this family, with varying numbers of dots on their backs. The convergent lady beetle is the one most commonly pictured and is the type purchased in quantity by organic gardeners from West Coast suppliers. It has 12 spots.

BRACONID WASP family Braconidae: This small parasitic wasp is not often noticed by gardeners, but it is an extremely important beneficial insect.

The female wasp lays its eggs on the larvae and pupae of butterflies and moths and on aphids, after which the host insect is slowly killed as its strength is sapped by the developing wasps. If you discover a caterpillar covered with tiny white spots or cocoons, do not remove it from the garden. The wasps will hatch out and continue their valuable work.

Similar beneficial insects are the trichogramma wasps, chalcid flies and ichneumen flies, some of which can be purchased through biological supply houses.

MANTIDS, praying mantids, family Mantidae: There are 20 species of praying mantids in North America, both green and brown in color.

The green Chinese mantid was introduced with a shipment of nursery stock from China in about 1895 and is one of the hardiest species.

Mantids are fearless and have been known to strike against frogs and lizards. They eat aphids, bees, hornets, each other and any other insect that passes within reach of their grasping forelegs.

Cases of 100 to 200 eggs may be purchased through the mail, but as with all beneficial insects, they move where the hunting is best.

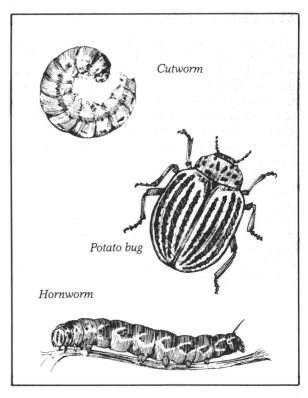

Cutworm

Potato bug

Hornworm

From Home Gardening Wisdom by Dick and Jan Raymond, published by Garden Way and available for $11.95 from Storey Communications, P.O. Box 105, Pownal, Vermont 05261.

WATER TABLES

Tomatoes need an adequate supply of water for vigorous, uniform growth. Moisture also assures the availability of soil nutrients. In a dry year, inadequate soil moisture upsets the calcium nutrition of tomato plants and tends to cause a greater incidence of blossom-end rot, a brown, water-soaked area that gradually develops into a black, sunken scar on the lower end of the tomato. Fruits also tend to be smaller in a dry year.

A uniform supply of moisture is particularly important at the time young fruits are developing on the first flower cluster. In a wet year, there is a greater incidence of uneven or blotchy ripening, growth cracking, fungal diseases and rotting of fruits, particularly those in contact with the soil. Susceptibility of tomato fruits to cracking largely depends on the variety.

As a general guide, tomato plants should receive one inch of water per week. If there is no rainfall for a week, water plants thoroughly. Heavy soakings at weekly intervals are better than several light sprinklings. Sandy soils need to be watered more often than clay and other heavy soils. Do not wet foliage any more than necessary, and do not water or spray tomatoes with a spray can that was used to apply 2,4-D; 2,4,5-T or related weed killers, since traces of these chemicals are extremely difficult to wash away. Tomatoes are very susceptible to injury by these chemicals, even from spray or vapor drifts that may come from roadside spraying or spraying of neighbors' lawns.

— **Growing Garden Tomatoes**

Pots & Plans

From Baskets to Waterbeds

Growing tomatoes in outdoor gardens is certainly the best way to harvest inexpensive fruit in great quantity. But it is not always a preferred or even possible way to go. Fortunately, there are alternative ways to grow tomatoes: outdoors in pots or boxes; in a greenhouse; or even indoors, either under lights or by a very sunny window. Some such plants are grown hydroponically, without soil. As long as they receive sufficient light, warmth, nutrients and water, and as long as a helpful hand ensures that the flowers are pollinated, tomatoes will set and ripen fruit anywhere. Such plants may provide the gardener with fruit out of season or out of place. For the innovative and the desperate, the rewards of indoor and container-grown tomatoes are especially sweet.

— JB

HIGH-RISE HORTICULTURE

Witold Rybczynski, professor of architecture at McGill University, headed a rooftop vegetable-

94

Small-fruited plants such as ornamental peppers and determinate cherry tomatoes occupy little space when grown in pots.

growing project in Montreal in 1975. The McGill project utilized wooden boxes, measuring about two feet by three feet and two feet deep. Good drainage was promoted by lining the bottoms with a half-inch layer of peat moss and vermiculite. The rooftop gardeners reported the best results when they planted just a single zucchini or broccoli to a box, two tomatoes or eggplants or three miniature cabbages planted in a triangle. Such a box will accommodate three rows of peas and two of beans, or it can be broadcast-seeded with carrots or lettuce (which are later thinned to leave two or three inches of space around each seedling).

Helga and William Olkowski, authors of *The City People's Book of Raising Food*, found that "with all the plants we tried, the larger the containers, the bigger the harvest. Tomatoes are particularly responsive to root depth. In our experience, the plant in the largest container will invariably live the longest and produce the most food." They decided that herbs and cherry tomatoes would tolerate a minimum of six inches of soil depth; radishes, lettuce and baby carrots could be planted in six inches but preferred eight; standard tomatoes, broccoli and cucumbers needed a bare minimum of one foot.

Whatever the container, proper drainage must be provided to avoid having water accumulate and initiate root decay. If a double-pot system is used (a container with drainage holes or spaces inside a nonleaking container), the bottom of the larger container should be covered with peat moss or vermiculite so that the inner pot can drain into the space below.

Wooden crates, used alone, are often leaky enough to eliminate the need to drill drainage holes. (One high-rise gardener set a routine of watering in the very early morning so that the tenants downstairs wouldn't see water streaking from her balcony down their outside wall.)

If possible, the containers should be filled with a mix containing rich topsoil from a ground-level gardener or farmer. Potting soil from a supermarket can be good or it can be poor, but it is always expensive. If gathering soil on an excursion to the countryside, avoid the temptation to take any material from the side of a busy road. Such earth is inevitably contaminated with the heavy metals lead and cadmium and thus is unsafe for use in growing vegetables.

To help lighten the weight load — both for carrying and to avoid detaching balcony from building — soil is usually mixed with peat moss, perlite or vermiculite (expanded volcanic material and puffed mica, respectively). These substances also serve to improve the texture of the soil, which is unlikely to have the benefit of earthworms or decomposing or-

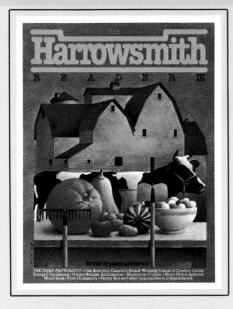

A Special Offer

The Best of Harrowsmith

The Harrowsmith Reader III preserves some of the best and most useful material from the Canadian edition of **Harrowsmith** magazine. Invaluable information on gardening, rural living, owner-builder architecture, wood heat, solar energy, small-stock husbandry, folk arts and natural cooking. Three hundred and twenty pages of pragmatic alternatives and great reading.

~~$16.95~~ NOW ONLY **$9.95**

Full-color throughout
Large-format softcover • 320 pages

To receive your copy of **The Harrowsmith Reader III**, fill in the convenient order form on the reverse side of this card, place in an envelope together with your payment, and mail to: **Harrowsmith Books,** The Creamery, Charlotte, Vermont 05445.

Harrowsmith Books

YES. Please send my copy of **The Harrowsmith Reader III.** I enclose payment of $9.95 per copy plus $1.50 to cover shipping and handling.

Name _____

Street _____

Town_____

State _____ Zip _____

Place this card in an envelope together with your payment, and mail to: **Harrowsmith Books,** The Creamery, Charlotte, Vermont 05445.

SATISFACTION GUARANTEED

Cherry tomatoes will tolerate a minimum soil depth of six inches but do better in more; standard tomatoes require a foot.

ganic matter to aerate the soil.

A full-fledged balcony garden could easily destroy the composure of most high-rise architects, and it is wise to keep in mind the fact that a cubic foot of soil weighs roughly 25 pounds, and most balconies are built to bear a maximum of 55 pounds per square foot. To avoid undue stress, place large containers against the wall, and do not build rooftop grow boxes without first investigating the strength of the roof supports.

Through trial and error, the Montreal group found that the ideal soil mix was seven parts topsoil and one part composed of equal portions of peat moss, vermiculite and perlite. The peat and vermiculite tend to hold moisture, the perlite promotes good drainage, and all three lighten the load.

Rybczynski's group discovered that plant growth and production were measurably improved with regular feedings of organic fertilizer every third week. Their combination included bone meal, granite dust, flaked seaweed, blood meal and liquid fish emulsion. A cheaper substitute would be a manure tea, made by soaking a cheesecloth bag filled with cow or horse manure, or perhaps a rich compost, in water overnight. The resulting fluid offers the plants an array of nutrients in a readily available form, and the remaining solid waste is mixed into the soil.

Bush-type plants with small tomatoes, such as **97**

Tiny Tim cherry tomatoes, or climbing small-fruited varieties like *Sweet 100* are ideal for high-rise culture. Patricia Rogal figures that because her balcony receives only four hours of sunshine daily in midsummer, her *Tiny Tim*s take longer to begin producing than the usual 45 days, but they still manage to develop ample fruit for salads during August and September. Larger tomatoes, although more difficult to grow, are tempting. Choose an early variety like *Moira*, a dwarf bush beefsteak, the first year, and see if conditions are favorable enough on your balcony to allow larger fruits to mature.

Watering, which commences as soon as the soil is mixed and continues, sometimes daily, until frost kills the most tender plants, is critical and even defeats some city high-risers. Mary Warkentin tried to grow tomatoes and herbs on her city balcony one summer but was discouraged after a weekend away from her apartment. "The plants were scorched," she says. "Having a garden is like having a cat or a dog. You have to be there all the time." Nevertheless, most apartment owners are able to coerce a friend into watering on the occasional weekend, and the gardener who finds he must neglect his plants for a few days can take precautions. Water in early morning or late evening—whenever the sun is not striking the plants—and then enclose the pot (but not the plant) in a plastic bag or sheets of plastic, covering as much of the soil as possible. Sheets or mats can be hung and secured on the sides of the balcony to reduce exposure to the sun and wind. Or if the plants are not too large, they can be moved indoors for the gardener's holiday.

In the meantime, a special connection from the kitchen sink to the balcony will make watering easier. (See Sources.) Watering must be very thorough to assure that the soil is saturated enough for water to seep out of the bottom of the pot after each session. When the soil surface is dry, in the case of seeds or seedlings, or, for larger plants, when the top half-inch is dry, it is time to water. Use water that is at room temperature, particularly on sensitive seeds and seedlings.

When the produce is ready for the table, the city gardener should take care to wash all vegetables. He may have been scrupulous in not using sprays on his plants, but unfortunately, city air can be laden with chemicals of its own. Lead levels, in particular, can be high in city-grown produce, especially if it is grown very close to a busy street or in the path of polluted exhausts. If your balcony is receiving a regular coating of soot or other pollutants, you may want to follow the directions suggested by the Institute for Local Self-Reliance in Washington, D.C., which has been doing tests on its own city-grown vegetables. Fruiting crops such as tomatoes, peppers and cucumbers, they say, accumulate the least lead, with root crops and leafy crops attaining respectively more. As younger plants are the most contaminant-free, plant and harvest frequently. Apparently, better soil quality also helps the plant resist lead accumulation.

— *Harrowsmith Staff*

TOMATO MATCHMAKERS

T he tomato, like the pepper, pea and most tree fruits, is an example of a "hermaphroditic" plant, one whose flowers each contain both female and male parts. These flowers are called "perfect," or complete.

The perfect-flowered vegetables are the most easily pollinated in the greenhouse. Tomatoes, peppers, beans and eggplants are often pollinated without the gardener's help or knowledge. The action of picking fruit, brushing against plants, moving plant pots or allowing a gust of air to blow through the greenhouse door may be enough to knock pollen onto the waiting stigmas. In fact, they self-pollinate so readily that the horticulturist who would control their breeding must go to some length to stop them. As Robert Harris, developer of the *Sub-Arctic Maxi* and *Sub-Arctic Cherry* tomatoes, explains, "As soon as

you see any color of flower in the female plant that you want, you remove all its anthers." (Anthers, containing the pollen grains, are at the top of the stamens, the male sex organs.) As part of the process of developing a new hybrid, the female is then fertilized with the desired male. This careful removal of the tiny anthers at the top of the stamens "is not much of a job," says Harris. "You can do quite a few in a short time."

Flowers normally release their pollen on warm, sunny days — the sort of weather that would bring out the bees — so there is not much point in pollinating on days when the sun never appears between the clouds. A bright day, between 10 a.m. and 2 p.m., when the blossoms are dry, is the right time for pollination. As long as flowers are blooming on the plants, they should be pollinated, which may mean attending to them every day for weeks at a time.

ELECTRIC BEES

Some greenhouse growers recommend suspending potted tomato plants from the roof of the greenhouse. This saves floor space and also makes the swaying and jostling, and consequent pollination, of plants likely.

Commercial greenhouses employ automatic bees and automatic wind to help their tomatoes along. An "electric bee" is a small hand-held instrument that physically touches the stem of each cluster of flowers, vibrating them so that pollen is shaken onto the stigma of each flower. Larger operations use an air blaster, which the operator carries on his back. This sends out torrents of air, tossing the plants enough to effect pollination. Very large, advanced operations train their tomato plants up wires attached to an overhead, lateral wire that vibrates periodically, shaking loose the pollen.

George (Doc) and Katy Abraham, who have two greenhouses in Naples, New York, and are authors of *Organic Gardening Under Glass*, solve most of their pollination problems by having a fan in the greenhouse. (Theirs is permanently installed, but some growers carry a portable fan around the greenhouse.)

Gardeners who want to be absolutely sure that pollination occurs, says Katy, should hand-pollinate their tomatoes, peppers and eggplants, touching each flower with the tip of a camel's-hair paintbrush.

— JB

HANGING BASKETS

Extension horticulturists at Michigan State University suggest that gardeners who want to grow tomatoes in hanging baskets start with one of the small-fruited, small-vined tomatoes such as *Small Fry* or *Patio*. (*Sweet 100* and other indeterminate varieties will grow too large for a hanging basket.) Most gardeners will want only a couple of hanging plants, so they may find it easier to buy them than to grow their own plants from seed.

Clay flowerpots or plastic, gallon-sized milk bottles make good hanging baskets. Almost any container can be used, however, as long as it holds at least four quarts of soil and can have several holes in the bottom for drainage. If the plant will be grown indoors, a drip catcher such as a clay saucer or an aluminum pie pan will be needed as well. A macrame pot hanger or a mesh onion bag can be used to suspend the container from a bracket or eye bolt.

The horticulturists recommend the use of commercially prepared potting soil in hanging baskets. Garden soil tends to drain very poorly, and it usually contains disease organisms and often insects that can be troublesome to container-grown plants. Line the bottom of the container with an inch of gravel, charcoal or pieces of broken clay pot. Mix some low-nitrogen, organic fertilizer with the soil, and fill the container to within one inch of the top with the soil mix. Water and settle the soil, and then add more soil if necessary.

Before removing it from its container, water the tomato transplant. Then hold it upside down with

Compact, small-fruited tomatoes such as Small Fry, Patio *and* Toy Boy *(above) are especially well suited to hanging baskets.*

the stem between your fingers, and tap the container gently against the edge of a table until the soil ball comes loose. Make a hole in the prepared soil big enough to hold the root ball, and insert the plant, firming the soil around it.

Place the container where the plant will receive as much direct sunlight as possible, six hours a day if possible. Plenty of sunlight is necessary for good flower and fruit production. A plant that receives light from only one direction should be turned occasionally so all sides are exposed to the light.

Check the soil frequently, and water as needed to keep the plant from wilting. The smaller the pot, the more frequently it will need water. After the plant has begun to set fruit, feed it with manure tea or a diluted seaweed or fish fertilizer.

Depending on the variety, its size and the availability of sunlight, tomatoes should ripen within 7 to 10 weeks from transplanting. In the fall, bring the plant indoors before it is killed by frost. Hang it in a sunny window so that any remaining tomatoes can ripen, or pick the fruits off and let them ripen on the windowsill. Then discard the plant. Because of low indoor light levels in the winter, there is little chance that it will survive long as a houseplant, let alone flower and produce fruit.

— *Michigan State University Information Services*

SUNNY CEILINGS

Optimistic articles in magazines often recommend growing entire salads on a "sunny windowsill." This has never worked for me. A couple of years ago, inspired by just such an article, we dug up two *Tiny Tims* well before the first frost, acclimatized them lovingly to the indoor atmosphere, cherished and coddled them on our sunniest windowsill, and they were dead before Christmas. Unanimous verdict: house too cold, daylight too short, tomatoes do not like being dug up when mature. That would probably have been the end of wintertime horticulture, except that last summer, an alien tomato plant sprang from the kitchen debris buried in our bean patch, roared up the closest bean pole, 6½ feet tall, and settled down to producing vast quantities of small tomatoes with delicious flavor all their own. It would have been heartless to abandon this prodigy to an Ontario winter; it was too huge to transplant, but a couple of six-inch cuttings rooted quickly in jam jars and when planted in large milk cartons grew quickly into two-foot plants. Unlike the unfortunate *Tiny Tims*, the unknown showed no signs of dying, but the foliage was pale, the plants lanky, and the flowers withered while barely past the bud stage.

Scientific sampling (leaving a room thermometer lying around in various places) showed that the only "hot spot" in this chilly residence occurs high up in the kitchen ceiling, where sunshine, cooking heat, steam from dishes sitting in a sudsy sink and a certain amount of warmth rising from the refrigerator coils combine to maintain a steady 70 degrees. So much for temperature. Rationalizing the cost with the excuse that we had always needed a light over the sink, we installed a light fixture, two 48-inch cool-white fluorescent tubes and two 15-watt incandescent bulbs high in the ceiling. Dangling below on a polystyrene tray and enjoying a 16-hour "day," our two unknown tomatoes, well cut back, are now putting out masses of genuine dark green tomato foliage and a few yellow flowers. Beside them, young *Grand Rapids* lettuces are rampant. I do not expect success this winter; but *next year*, with cuttings taken from small, well-behaved *Tiny Tim* plants hanging high in the kitchen, I fully expect that we shall have our own version of their "sunny windowsill salad bowl."

— *Jean Cameron*

VEGETABLES IN THE BAG

It is doubtful that they will ever replace the aesthetically pleasing terra cotta clay pot as a gardener's delight, but horticultural growing bags are fast gaining acceptance in commercial greenhouses and are expected to make quick inroads among indoor and patio vegetable gardeners.

More than 90 percent of the Irish tomato crop is now grown in plastic bags (typically 44 inches long, 14 inches wide and containing 1.5 cubic feet of compost, with three plants per sack), following tests that showed production increases of 50 percent or more per acre. The low-cost bags minimize the effects of soil-borne diseases and parasites, such as fusarium, verticillium and nematodes, and end the need for growers to steam-sterilize greenhouse soil beds.

According to Dr. Ray Sheldrake, professor emeritus of Cornell University, bag horticulture also holds great promise for "gardeners surrounded by concrete."

TOMATOES WITHOUT SOIL

It was one of those wretched mornings in late February, with lake winds whipping the snow off my driveway only to reveal a glaze of fresh ice. While the radio weatherman was making dire predictions of more freezing rain and warning motorists about the abysmal winter driving conditions, I picked the last of five fully vine-ripened tomatoes in my basement. Dozens more hung on the vines, oblivious to the storm and promising many harvests yet to come.

Here, the fluorescent lights were cheerful, and the smell of growing plants and the warmth of the room seemed proof that my colleague, Steve Tobe, had introduced me to the perfect formula for endless summer. Seasons removed from the whirling snow outside, the pumps of my hydroponic unit cut in. I watched, through the tangle of green foliage, as the gravel bed slowly darkened with moisture, and then I heard the nutrient solution trickling back into the reservoir under the gravel.

"No doubt about it," I thought, sampling a sweet, juicy *Starshot* tomato, "hydroponic gardening can change your whole outlook on winter."

It will come as no surprise to anyone who witnesses this near miracle of displaced summer that hydroponics made possible one of the Seven Wonders of the World. The Hanging Gardens of Babylon grew, some say, hydroponically, much as the jungle of suspended houseplants at Steve's place grows today.

King Nebuchadnezzar II's amazing gardens thrilled travellers centuries before the term hydroponics was coined. Derived from two Greek words – *hydro* (water) and *ponos* (labor) – the system is essentially soilless horticulture. As practiced in the early 20th century, the root system of a plant was suspended in a solution of water containing all of the known essential plant nutrients.

The usual modern practice is to grow the plant in an inert aggregate of gravel or vermiculite (puffed granules of mica ore) and to pump a nutrient solution through this several times a day at preset intervals of the light cycle. This aggregate serves to support the root system and – since the nutrient solution does not bathe the roots continuously – allows oxygen, necessary for plant growth, to reach the roots more easily.

Proponents of organic gardening are often suspicious of hydroponic culture, citing the use of chemical fertilizers and growing conditions that obviously are not natural. Hydroponic systems are not for everyone, but the fact is that nutrient solutions comprised of fish emulsion, liquid seaweed and blood meal can be used if one wishes to be strictly organic.

Whether organic or not, whether grown in soil or hydroponically, all plants require proper light for healthy growth and highest yields. In addition to the proper nutrient solution, the plants need carbon dioxide and oxygen from the air, as well as proper temperature conditions and a good supporting medium, one that will allow adequate aeration for the roots, especially at the crown.

In a hydroponic system, all these needs must be satisfied manually or automatically, and they must be supplied within a closed system. The basic components of any hydroponic unit are: a container, the aggregate, the nutrient solution, the reservoir and lights. An automated system requires a small water pump and a timer to activate the lights and pumping system.

Virtually any container that does not leak and will not rot can be used for a hydroponic garden. Hydroponic planters vary from plant pots or simple porch hangers to entire greenhouses. The most basic type of container that we have found practical is the common dishpan – ideal for the cautious neophyte or for those who wish to take advantage of south-facing windows that would not accommodate larger tanks. We have used these 11-by-13-inch Rubbermaid-type dishpans to grow a variety of vegetables, including tomatoes, English cucumbers, green beans, lettuce and watercress.

GRAVEL

DISHPAN
FITTED WITH DRAINAGE SPOUT

In soil, tomato roots reach very deep, but because all the plant's nutritional needs are met in the richly fed aggregate, hydroponic root systems are small. I have grown a 10-foot-high tomato plant in such a container. Normally, a dishpan will hold one large plant (a tomato or cucumber or pepper) or two small ones (herbs or lettuce).

With this type of container, it is necessary to install a spout on the side of the pan near the bottom, or simply drill a hole and fit it with a cork or rubber stopper to provide drainage. The aggregate is flooded with nutrients once or twice a day, and the solution is allowed to drain out, after the appropriate time, through the spout or drainage hole. With all the systems described in this article, the nutrient solution will be poured on the aggregate either manually or by electric pump, and then the solution will drain back into the reservoir by itself, using gravity.

The container must now be filled with the growing medium, or aggregate. The most commonly used aggregate is gravel, usually ⅜-inch size or finer, and well cleaned. Impurities on the gravel, such as clay or soil, can affect the pH of the medium quite dramatically and also may contain minerals that will upset the nutrient balance. We have used gravel successfully in both large and small containers and consider it to be the cheapest and most reliable growing medium. The least expensive is available

105

from a building supplier and is often called "pea" gravel. However, this gravel is usually "contaminated" with clay and must be washed until the water runs clear before being used as a hydroponic aggregate.

Commercially available hydroponic aggregates, which require no cleaning, consist of porous rock and come in 25-pound bags under such trade names as Heylite and Herculite. Because they are prewashed and ready for use in the tanks, they are relatively expensive. Nonetheless, this porous aggregate appears to have two advantages. It retains the water better than ordinary gravel and provides a greater surface area for root growth. We have had excellent results with both gravel and porous rock and leave it to the reader to decide which aggregate to use.

The major problem with gravel as the growing medium is its weight. A large tank filled with gravel weighs several hundred pounds and is very difficult to move. If portability is desired, lighter materials for aggregates can be used. The two most commonly available materials are vermiculite and perlite. We have used both of these materials successfully, although they have several disadvantages. They tend to retain salts on their surfaces and must be backwashed to remove these salts at regular intervals. Because of their lightness, plants may require ex-

ternal support, and because these materials retain excessive moisture due to their large surface area, algae and fungi tend to grow on them, and insufficient oxygen may reach the plant roots, causing rot.

The water-retaining characteristics of vermiculite and perlite can, however, be used to advantage. We have obtained excellent results by combining one of these materials with gravel, thereby utilizing the best qualities of each. We make a sort of gravel sandwich in the large tank by placing a one-inch layer of gravel in the bottom, on the aggregate platform, covering this with a one- or two-inch layer of vermiculite or perlite and then adding three or four additional inches of gravel. We now use this mixture routinely in our hydroponic tanks. The same system — with thinner layers — can be used in a dishpan, although it is easiest to use only one aggregate in these. If I use vermiculite in a dishpan, I put a bit of gravel over the drainage hole so that the finer aggregate will not flow out.

NUTRIENT SOLUTIONS

Nutrient solutions are really a matter of personal taste — "organic" versus "inorganic." We have used both types successfully but have discontinued using the organic solutions because of the ripe odor they create (essence of dead fish, ripe seaweed and blood meal). We offer two nutrient formulations

POTTED PIXIES

Seba Beach is a summer village about 50 miles west of Edmonton. Our house is on the lakeshore, and as a result, we are a little slow to warm up in the spring but manage to miss the first few frosts in the fall. This year, Mother Nature saw fit to dump seven inches of snow on us on October 17.

I am not a hot-shot gardener by any means, but I have had good success with *Pixie* hybrid tomatoes. I grow them in three-gallon plastic pails, which I get from the local bakery. From an April 1 start in a warm window, vine-ripened fruit is ready to eat by the third week in July. They yield until frost finally gets them, when I get too lazy to put them in the house on cold nights. They yield small fruit, about two inches across, but in this country, the game is to have ripe tomatoes, not large green ones, when frost hits.

— *Jim McIntyre*

but, at the risk of precipitating a controversy, must say that the so-called "organic/natural" mixture utilizes processed compounds and is probably no more organic than the straight salt mixture, the components of which can be mined directly from the ground with little processing.

Plants cannot take up organic matter directly; they can only absorb inorganic molecules. Organic materials such as compost or manure must break down into various inorganic components before they can be taken up by the plant as nutrients — as far as the plant is concerned, there is no difference. Those who advocate purely organic practices, of course, claim that seaweed, fish emulsion and other "natural" fertilizers contain trace elements that are neither measurable nor completely understood yet. We leave the choice up to you.

Inorganic Salt Mixture
11½ oz. ammonium sulphate
8 oz. ammonium phosphate
4 oz. potassium chloride
3 oz. calcium sulphate
5½ oz. magnesium sulphate

Mix well and use 1 to 2 tsp. per gallon of water.

Organic Mixture
(from Institute for Local Self-Reliance)

1½ tsp. fish emulsion
1½ tsp. liquid seaweed
1 tsp. blood meal
1 gal. water

We have listed the inorganic mixture primarily so that the ingredients can be examined. It is very difficult for someone without access to chemicals to obtain the necessary individual salts, although some hydroponic greenhouses may be willing to sell small quantities. The organic mixture must be made by the gardener.

We feel that the most practical answer for the individual who does not mind using a chemical fertilizer is a commercial hydroponic mixture. We have used the formulation sold as City Green with good results and recommend it. It is unnecessary to use trace elements, as they are already present. All the salt mixtures are used at the rate of approximately one or two tablespoons in four gallons of water. Exceeding this rate appreciably will upset the nutrient balance of the solution. As the water level in the reservoir drops because of evaporation and transpiration, add more water (*not* nutrient solution) — we usually add water once or twice a week, never letting the water level drop below about 80 percent of the original volume. We usually check the pH of the nutrient solution every two weeks. This is simply a measure of the acidity or alkalinity of the solution, and for most plants that we have grown, the ideal pH is around 6 to 6.5. If the pH drops much below this (that is, if the solution becomes more acidic), it indicates that microorganisms have been at work, and the nutrient solution should be changed immediately. Plants grown at too acid a pH show flower drop and yellowing leaves. Litmus, or pH paper, can be obtained from many seed houses and garden supply shops.

We usually add nutrients once every three or four weeks. It is difficult to specify exactly how often nutrients should be added because this depends upon the number and type of plants being grown. The rate of nutrient addition is determined by experimentation. As a rough guide, one or two tablespoons of "inorganic" or "organic" mixture every three or four weeks should be ample for an eight-square-foot tank containing a full complement of actively growing plants.

As a final note, the nutrient solution should be changed regularly, about every four months. In the large tanks, the old solution must be siphoned off — not the most pleasant job in the world, but the slightly salty taste of the solution, should the siphoner get a mouthful, is not too objectionable. The aggregate is then washed off with 5 to 10 gallons of water and siphoned off again, and new nutrient solution is introduced. This process cleans adhering salts off the aggregate. The same process must be followed with the dishpan containers, but siphoning will not be required.

Greenhouse tomatoes are grown either hydroponically or in soil, above.

FEEDING

Having the properly balanced nutrient solution sitting in a reservoir may be commendable, but it must get to the aggregate to do the plants any good. The cheapest method can be employed with the dishpans. The gardener simply pours the solution onto the aggregate twice a day (or three times if the plants wilt frequently), leaves the solution there for about 15 minutes and then removes the stopper or opens the spout, allowing the solution to drain back into the reservoir. Such a manual system will, of course, require that somebody be available at least twice a day to service the plants.

We have some advice concerning the dishpan system, either manual or automatic. The pans should be slightly inclined, with the spout lower than the other end of the pan. This will facilitate drainage of the nutrient solution back to the reservoir.

The type of vegetable being grown will dictate temperature and light requirements. Warm-temperature crops such as peppers, tomatoes and cucumbers require an ambient daytime temperature of at least 75 to 80 degrees F, whereas cool-weather crops such as lettuce and spinach prefer a daytime temperature of 65 to 70 degrees. In a typical house, it is fairly easy to find this range of temperatures, particularly as the lights will radiate a considerable amount of heat. Nighttime temperatures will be the

109

most critical in houses that are not centrally heated.

We grow lettuce and spinach in an unfinished basement, where the temperature stays around 65 degrees F, and grow our tomatoes, peppers and cucumbers in a small upstairs room close to a radiator. When the fluorescent lights are on, the temperature in the room reaches 85 degrees. For good fruit set and growth of tomatoes and peppers, it is important to provide plants with these higher temperatures.

Light requirements also vary, depending upon the crop. Tomatoes, peppers and cucumbers prefer high light intensities, whereas lettuce, spinach and many herbs such as chervil and parsley can be grown at much lower light intensities. Clearly, plants that require higher temperatures also generally require the most light.

But almost all plants will require the installation of fluorescent fixtures, *even if the tank is located in a south-facing window*. Light from the sun is simply not enough, particularly during the winter. No matter what the circumstances, the plants should have 14 or 15 hours of light a day.

We provide light from Cool-Lite fluorescent tubes at the rate of eight 40-watt tubes (four-foot tubes) per eight-square-foot tank for our crops that require a lot of light, and four to six such tubes for lower light requirements. Light from windows will decrease the amount of artificial light needed, but it will al-ways be necessary to provide such light from 5 to 8 a.m. and from 4 to 8 p.m. The importance of adequate light cannot be overemphasized. It is the single most important factor limiting the number of plants that can be grown in a unit. Watch the plants for spindly growth and poor fruit set — indicators of insufficient light.

FORT SMITH HYDROPONICS

Our first experiment with hydroponics was in 26 feet of eaves troughing. Twelve celery plants, eight tomatoes, six zucchini and a few nasturtiums were grown in a four-inch depth of pea gravel, a little charcoal and a shovelful of peat moss. From very little nutrient, there came a tremendous reward.

Also, seven *Pixie* tomatoes sat in pots on the front step, and they had 120 ripening fruit by the middle of August.

— *Ray Schmidt*
Fort Smith, Northwest Territories

Four-foot-long four-tube fluorescent fixtures are the most convenient source of artificial illumination. We have mounted ours on chains or ropes so that their height can be adjusted as the plants grow. We usually locate the lights about one foot from the surface of the aggregate and, as the plants grow, raise the lights. However, when the lights reach 2½ to 3 feet above the aggregate, it is time to start cutting back the plants rather than raising the lights further. Our lighting system is connected to a timer so that daily maintenance of the units is minimized.

SEED VARIETIES

Plants that keep bumping into the lights or threaten to turn the living room into the perfect setting for Martin Denny music are probably not the best varieties for hydroponic use. Ideal hydroponic plants will not grow too large too fast; they will put their energy into fruiting. Seed catalogues are not geared to such varieties, and so it is often difficult to choose the right varieties for one's particular needs, and experimentation is the only way to find the answer.

We have been experimenting with suitable varieties for hydroponic culture for three years and can offer some advice on which ones seem to grow particularly well. For germinating tomato, pepper and herb seeds, we use Jiffy Pots, which are placed in the aggregate after the seedlings sprout. Lettuce seed can be planted right on the surface of the aggregate and pressed in slightly. Cucumber, bean and spinach seeds should be covered with a little aggregate.

The two varieties of tomatoes that we recommend most highly for growing and for eating are *Starshot* and *Stakeless*. These varieties are small and stocky and set lots of fruit — ideal for hydroponic culture. The small-fruited *Starshot* mature well before the larger-fruited *Stakeless*, and by regular planting of these two varieties, we have a continuous supply of tomatoes. One should have no difficulty getting 20 to 40 fruits per *Starshot* plant.

Clearly, for us, hydroponic gardening is an ongoing process of experimentation and discovery. We usually find that people are quite skeptical about our claims — that yields are very high, that the fruit tastes sweet and delicious — and yet we have proved these things to our own satisfaction, as scientists, time and time again. The rewards of hydroponic gardening are tremendous. One of the nicest Christmas presents we know of is a vine-ripened pesticide-free tomato — it is guaranteed to take the chill from the worst weather that winter can bring.

— *Dr. Stephen Tobe & Dr. William Friend*

The Harvest Bounty

A Time to Reap

Anyone who has as much trouble imagining a hamburger without catsup as picturing spaghetti without Ragu will scarcely wonder at the tomato's status as the most frequently consumed of North American vegetables. Although it is often disguised, the peripatetic tomato contributes more vitamins to our diet than does any other vegetable, even ones like broccoli or spinach that are considerably more nutritious. In some gardeners' households, tomatoes are virtually a staple winter food, filling entire cupboards with sparkling quart and pint jars of tomato sauce, tomato paste and stewed tomatoes that will add color, nutrients and flavor to an amazing variety of dishes.

This versatility and wholesomeness also encourages gardeners to have faith in tomatoes, to grow as many as possible and to prolong the harvest as long as possible by choosing fast-maturing tomatoes and protecting them from early fall frosts. When the homemade catsup and spaghetti sauces are stored safely for winter, there is still enough fruit left for those standbys of the gardener's kitchen: spicy chili sauce, green tomato mincemeat and whole, frozen tomatoes.

— JB

In the United States, more than 1.4 million tons of tomatoes are produced for fresh market sale each year.

FROST PROTECTION

"Light freeze," "moderate freeze" and "severe freeze" or "killer frost," are some of the terms gardeners, eyes heavenward, bandy over the late-ripening tomatoes. A light freeze is defined as a drop to 32 degrees F, a moderate freeze is 29 degrees and a severe freeze 25 degrees. The vague term "killer frost" is defined as occurring "when the temperature in a screened cage four feet above the ground is 28 degrees F or lower." Such latitude is avoided by research scientists' far more precise referral to the LD-50 for any species of plant; that is, the temperature at which 50 percent of the specimens die. The United States Weather Bureau identifies frosts by the temperatures at which they occur: 32 degrees, 28 degrees, 24 degrees, 20 degrees and 16 degrees or lower, each point being especially important for at least one commercial crop. Cucumbers and tomatoes succumb to temperatures between 32 degrees and 38 degrees, beans and potatoes to 32 degrees, sweet corn and asparagus to 30 degrees.

The frost-free period of any area is generally defined as the number of calendar days between the last 32 degree F frost in the spring and the first one in the fall. Walla Walla, Washington, has an average frost-free season of 217 days; Syracuse, New York, has 168 days; Glasgow, Montana, 125 days.

This is not, however, the whole story. The growing season of any area may, with a little preparation by the gardener, extend several weeks beyond the frost-free season.

Many vegetables, as we have seen, will not be killed by a 32 degree F frost, and so the gardener's first line of defense against frost is crossed with his or her choice of crops. Beans are reduced to black rags after a frosty night, while the carrots and kale often stand proudly and greenly. The former are among the "tender" crops; carrots are dubbed "semi-hardy" and kale "frost-hardy." The latter is not immune to freezing, of course, but will survive a few degrees of frost while tender plants will not. Popular tender garden plants include snap and soybeans, tomatoes, peppers, eggplants, cucumbers, squash and melons.

In very short-season areas, tender crops should be grown in a greenhouse or not at all. In most gardens "north of 60," frost is quite possible at any time during the summer.

When a frost warning has been announced, or when the gardener observes the sign of approaching frost – a low temperature that rapidly drops after sunset – mechanical barriers, water and smoke can all be used to lessen frost damage. Of these, the easiest way to keep light frost off plants is simply to cover them. A cover contains the radiating heat

CORRUPTING INFLUENCES

These apples, as also the whole plant, chill the body, albeit less than does mandragora; wherefore it is dangerous to make use of them. Nevertheless, some do eat them cooked, with oil, salt and pepper. They give little nourishment to the body and that little bad and corrupt.

— *Dalechamps*
Histoire des Plantes, 1653

given off by the plants and prevents moisture from settling on the foliage and fruit. Just as pumpkins are protected from the first frost by a canopy of pumpkin leaves, so a covering of plastic, newspaper, bed sheets or almost anything similar can be effective. Double glazing is even better. Two layers of plastic spaced about two inches apart will give protection against about 5 degrees of frost — that is, down to about 27 degrees F.

Graham Saunders, who gardens in the Northeast, notes that "merely dragging plastic over the vegetables means that some of the leaves and vines will touch the plastic and freeze if some way of elevating the cover is not found." He drives stakes four or eight feet apart in the area of the garden reserved for tender plants.

"I have made frames measuring four by eight feet from 2x2 lumber, which is covered with heavy polyethylene and stapled. When it is likely to be colder than 41 degrees F, these covered frames go on the stakes in the evening." Saunders then drapes a large piece of black plastic over the frames to cover both top and sides. "Once the frames are built and the stakes are in position, it takes only a few minutes to set them up."

SPRINKLING FROST AWAY

As soon as the temperature rises above freezing in the morning, any covers should be removed. While such methods are inexpensive and effective in the home garden, all that covering and uncovering does demand time and manpower. Furthermore, the method is not suitable for large plants such as fruit trees, and without supplementary heat, it is not effective below 23 degrees F. For larger areas, larger plants or colder temperatures, sprinkler systems are sometimes employed.

The principle at work seems right out of *Through the Looking Glass*. As water freezes, it releases heat. If the ambient temperature is not too low, this released heat, constantly applied, can be sufficient to keep plants from freezing. Dr. G.H. Gubbels, who conducted sprinkler tests in the Yukon Territory, noted in the *Canadian Journal of Plant Science*, "No damage was apparent on any test plants due to stopping sprinkler irrigation when the control temperature rose above 32 degrees F, even though ice remained on the plants."

The drawbacks to the system include its requirements for large amounts of water and good sprinkling equipment. Sprinkling is commenced as soon as the temperature drops to freezing and must continue until after it has risen above freezing the next morning—too little water is worse than none at all.

Creating no such problems, but producing a few troublesome side effects of its own, is smoke, at one time a popular frost repellent. Surprisingly, it is not primarily the heat but the smoke itself that prevents frost damage in this case. Large smoke particles hinder the escape of longwave radiation from the earth and help keep the temperature up.

L.H. Bailey's *Cyclopedia of American Horticulture*, published in 1900, recommended that, in the home garden, fires be made in piles of matter as wet as possible: "Of home resources, damp straw or hay, loose manure, prunings of trees and other litter are among the best. It is essential that the piles be comparatively small and rather numerous. On level land, it is best to have these piles on all four sides of the area at a distance of not more than 10 to 30 feet apart. On

116

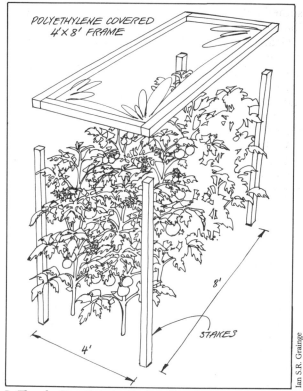

POLYETHYLENE COVERED 4' X 8' FRAME

8'

4'

STAKES

Ian S.R. Grainge

In Thunder Bay, Ontario, Graham Saunders rests plastic-covered wood frames on stakes, protecting tomatoes underneath.

somewhat steep slopes, the piles may be placed on the upper side . . . ."

Graham Saunders has utilized this method in his garden. "I used to start a fire just to the north of the garden when the temperature was still a few degrees above freezing. Every so often, I would place more wet hay on the fire, which released millions of smoke particles. One morning, the fog was so thick that a passing motorist had to put his lights on."

With increasingly stringent regulations against air pollutants and summer burning, such measures are not only annoying but also illegal in some places; smudge pots have been outlawed in American citrus-growing states since the '50s. Besides, the *Cyclopedia* notes, as frost usually occurs late at night, "It is best for a man to sit up and devote himself to the business." Most of us lack that sort of eye-watering dedication.

Gardeners who opt for the use of direct heat may also spend some sleepless nights, wondering if the fuel supply has run out or if the heater has tipped over, igniting the mulch. Effective but expensive, the use of heaters is now the chosen frost repellent of some commercial enterprises. Many small heaters are more effective than a few large ones.

Fans and even helicopters are also used by farmers in pursuit of a longer growing season. Such methods ´work by mixing very cold air near the ground with warmer air above it. On calm nights, minimum temperatures near ground level are often from 2 to 10 degrees F lower than those measured 4½ feet above the ground – where meteorological readings are normally made.

When fall days begin to cool, especially when a cold front has just passed and the weather reports threaten "frost in low-lying areas," harvesting becomes fast and frantic. Everything susceptible to damage is moved out of harm's way. Immature peppers, beans and summer squash can be eaten; tomatoes and melons will ripen somewhat indoors. Choose tomatoes that have already begun ripening, those that have a whitish appearance. Really green fruit will not ripen off the plant but can be used in recipes that call for them.

Mamie Munro, who gardens in the Northwest, reports that after she covered her tomato plants on several frosty nights, the harvest took place. "Finally on August 31 and September 2, we brought in 44 pounds of green tomatoes. With my father's guidance, we wrapped them in newspaper and left them on a table in the basement to ripen. By September 30, we commenced eating our own ripened tomatoes. I was quite surprised that they had a home-grown flavor, even though they had been picked green."

— Harrowsmith Staff **117**

PERPETUAL TOMATOES

Saving the seed from his or her own tomatoes is easy to do and ensures the gardener an endless supply of good-quality seed free of charge. But if the seed-saving process is to be successful, gardeners are always advised to follow certain guidelines, one of which is that the fruit be fully mature before it is picked for seed.

The fruit should also be nonhybrid. Hybrid tomato seeds, which are fortunately labelled as such in most seed catalogues, produce perfectly good plants, but the plants themselves produce seed that may or may not grow into a plant like the parent. More likely, the offspring will hark back to one of its more distant predecessors. Growing seed saved from hybrid plants is an interesting experiment, but it is not recommended for anyone who wants a sure crop next year.

Fortunately, there are many nonhybrid (or open-pollinated) tomato varieties on the market, including all the heirloom types offered by groups such as the Seed Savers Exchange in Decorah, Iowa, and most tomatoes produced by government or university plant breeders. The Ontario-bred *Coldset*, *Moira* and *Veeroma*, Manitoba-bred *Manitoba*, and hundreds more, are all nonhybrid and thus good candidates for home seed saving. Almost every gar-

den store seed rack and mail-order seed catalogue carries at least one or two nonhybrid tomatoes.

Any tomato the gardener does decide to grow for seed should be cultivated in relative isolation from other tomatoes. Tomato flowers are predominantly self-pollinating, so they are usually, in effect, both mother and father to their seeds, having eliminated outside genetic influences. But cross-pollination can occur, especially with some varieties and some weather conditions and where there are many wild bees. Dr. Jeff McCormack, director of the Southern Exposure Seed Exchange in North Garden, Virginia, suggests that in order to harvest fairly pure seed, the gardener should plant modern tomato varieties at least 10 feet apart and heirloom varieties, which are even more likely to cross-pollinate, 20 to 25 feet apart. Other types of vegetables can, of course, be planted between the different tomato varieties.

As the plants grow, Kent Whealy, founder of the Seed Savers Exchange, advises gardeners to "look at the whole plant. Select several plants to save seed from, not just the best-looking or largest one. This will give your seed a greater genetic diversity and the ability to adapt to a variety of conditions."

Whealy says that home gardeners and researchers should be especially aware of differences between plants. Note characteristics such as size of fruit, flavor, earliness, disease and insect resistance, drought resistance, vigor of growth, storability, ability to survive cold weather, and so forth. Then select fruit only from the plants that best display the qualities the gardener wants.

Once the gardener has picked ripe (if possible) fruit from the best plants, he should dig out the seeds with a spoon and put them in a glass. The jelly-like pulp will still surround them, but three days of fermentation in enough water to cover the seed-pulp mixture will separate the two. Stir at least twice daily. My wife and I have found that germination, which is not desired at this point, will begin to take place in about four days if the water is as warm as room temperature, but according to a booklet put out by Johnny's Selected Seeds (see *Sources*), seeds can be left in the water for four days without germination if the water temperature is 60 degrees F and only two days if the temperature is 80 degrees. Johnny's recommends the four days of cooler fermentation, if at all possible, because it has a greater effect on destroying the spores of disease organisms that may be lying dormant on the seed coat.

Once the seeds have settled to the bottom and the fermentation process has ended, pour off the pulp and peelings, add fresh, cool water, allow the seed to settle on the bottom again, pour off most of the liquid, and repeat the process until the seed is clean.

Dry your seed on either a fine-mesh screen or waxed paper. You will have to flip the seeds over to dry the other side if you place them on waxed paper. I use waxed paper and a fan that blows directly onto the seeds for 24 hours, but they can also be dried in the sun, by a wood stove or in an oven, as long as the temperature does not exceed 96 degrees

VICTORIAN ADVICE

We have known an enthusiastic Tomato grower save his crop from an untimely June frost by placing small heaps of shavings around his Tomato plantation on the north, east and west sides, and when the thermometer indicated the approach of frost, he would light his piles of shavings and rubbish on the windward side, and the wind would blow the warm smoke over the plot of ground and thus save the plants from the frost. In his locality, there was no danger of frost when the wind was in the south, hence he placed no heaps of combustibles on that side. In this manner, he has saved his crop of Tomatoes not once, nor twice, but several times, and as he usually plants an acre or more and markets the crop, it is quite a material item with him.

— *D.W. Beadle*
Canadian Fruit, Flower & Kitchen Gardener
1872

F. Excessive temperatures will kill the seeds.

Make sure your seeds are completely dry before you store them. There should be no feeling of dampness as you pick them up, nor should they appear swollen. A properly dried tomato seed will appear flat and almost desiccated. Once the seeds are dry, rub them between your hands to break them apart. Put each kind of tomato seed into its own envelope labelled with the variety name and the year of storage, and put the envelopes into an airtight tin or glass jar with a snap lid or rubber gasket lid that can be tightened enough to make it moisture proof. Black electrical tape can be wound around the lid if you are suspicious of leaks. Store the seeds at as low a temperature as possible; freezing will not harm them. These seeds should stay viable for at least four years.

— *Ronald Driskill*
Siberia Seeds

RED ALERT

These apples were eaten by some Italians like melons, but the strong stinking smell gives one sufficient notice how unhealthful and evil they are to eat.
— *Matthias de L'Obel, 1581*

UNRIPE IS BEAUTIFUL

Each September when I confront our garden and its frost-threatened crops, I get the panicky feeling that I am at the center of the green tomato capital of the universe.

There are tomatoes everywhere. Many are destined to become red, other low-acid varieties will mature as yellow or white fruits. In the meantime, they are all green. They are arranged decoratively in bowls and baskets on every available flat surface. They are wrapped individually in newspaper and hidden in brown paper bags to ripen slowly in a dark room. There are whole plants, bearing unripe tomatoes, hanging by their roots in the tool shed.

As they ripen, the reds and yellows are canned (for soups and sauces). I skin them by first dipping them in boiling water, then cooling in a cold bath. For freezing, I cut them in squares and package the wedges in waxed milk cartons, which are then labelled and stapled shut at the top.

Toward the end of the fall ripening period, the jars and milk cartons full of tomatoes make impressive rows under the sink or in the freezer. The warmth of the kitchen is now beginning to be appreciated and the clouds of canning steam forgotten for another year.

I turn to the laggards. They squat in the sun or

crouch in darkened rooms, defiant — as green and hard as they were the day we rushed to pick them before the first frost. There is the temptation to throw them at the moon, but frugality prevails.

While green tomatoes stocked away carefully will usually ripen right up until Christmas, there is no reason to wait. In fact, considering the versatility of unripened tomatoes, there is every reason to try them in the following recipes:

GREEN TOMATO PIE

This is an unusual treat, somewhat similar to a tart green apple pie, that can be served warm with Cheddar cheese, whipped cream or a scoop of ice cream.

Core and slice 4 cups green tomatoes. Combine: ½ cup white sugar, ½ cup brown sugar, ¼ cup corn syrup, ½ tsp. salt, 2 Tbsp. butter, 2 Tbsp. lemon juice, 1 tsp. grated lemon rind, 4 Tbsp. cornstarch, 1½ tsp. cinnamon, ½ tsp. ground nutmeg and ½ tsp. allspice.

Bring to a boil. Line a 9-inch pie pan with pastry, and fill with the sliced tomatoes. Pour the cooked mixture over them, and add the top crust. Crimp edges, and cut slits in the top. Bake at 375 degrees F on the bottom oven rack until the top crust is golden and the tomatoes tender (about 45 minutes).

GREEN TOMATO CURRY

To make the base:

Sauté a large minced onion in 2 Tbsp. butter. Add 4 large green tomatoes, chopped. Cover and simmer until tomatoes soften. Sprinkle approximately 4 Tbsp. flour and 2 tsp. (or more) curry powder, salt, pepper, a pinch of sugar and cardamom (optional) over the partially cooked tomatoes.

Stir thoroughly, add 2 cups water (or broth), and simmer until thick. Taste and adjust spices.

Add any of the following, and heat through: cooked, cubed lamb, beef, pork, chicken livers; sliced hard-boiled eggs; shrimp.

Serve with steaming rice and condiments or on toast. Serves 6.

FRIED GREEN TOMATOES

This specialty has a following all its own, and one measure of a greasy spoon is whether you can get a side order of fried green tomatoes with breakfast.

Cut green tomatoes in thick slices, then dredge in flour or cornmeal that has been seasoned with salt, pepper and a trace of white or brown sugar.

Pan-fry in 2 Tbsp. butter until crisp and golden on both sides. For special occasions, try adding sour cream to the pan juices, heat, season and pour over the tomatoes.

This recipe also works well with red tomatoes. **121**

GREEN TOMATO MINCEMEAT

This mincemeat is not only superb in pies and tarts but special when heated, set aflame with brandy and poured over ice cream.

3 lbs. green tomatoes, chopped
3 lbs. tart apples, peeled, cored and chopped
2½ lbs. brown sugar
1 lb. seedless raisins
1 cup of suet, finely chopped
½ cup vinegar
1 Tbsp. each: cinnamon, cloves, nutmeg, allspice, salt

Combine all ingredients, and bring slowly to the boiling point. Reduce heat, and simmer until quite thick.

Option: Omit the suet, and stir in ¾ cup butter after the mincemeat has simmered.

GREEN TOMATO CATSUP

8 lbs. green tomatoes
1 green pepper
2 lbs. onions
½ cup pickling salt
1½ quarts cider vinegar
3½ lbs. sugar

In a tightly woven spice bag:

FROSTY FRUIT

I'd like to pass along my method for freezing tomatoes. It is a time and energy saver and is especially good for the cherry types. Simply rinse, dry and pop into the freezer. When frozen, put them into freezer bags. When you want to use them, simply drop them in cold water for a minute, and the skins come off ever more easily than with blanching. Or they can be left whole — I have used frozen cherry tomatoes in salads, putting them in at the last and just when they are completely thawed. They can also be used for sauce, soup, stewed tomatoes and wherever one would use canned tomatoes.

— *Mary Small*

1 tsp. cinnamon
1 tsp. powdered cloves
½ tsp. cayenne

Wash and stem tomatoes and green pepper. Chop onions, tomatoes and green pepper coarsely, and soak overnight in pickling salt. Drain and rinse. Measure tomato mixture, and place in a kettle with an equal amount of water plus 1 pint of vinegar.

The commercial alternative to home preserves comes from tons of Ontario tomatoes awaiting processing by Heinz.   **123**

Cook for 1 hour, making sure that the tomatoes are cooked through. Remove from heat and drain.

Boil the sugar, 1 quart of vinegar and the spices for 1 hour. Let cool, and mix with the cooked, drained tomatoes. Pack in clean, hot jars and seal.

Makes 4 to 6 quarts.

— *Nancy Martin*

WHOLE CANNED TOMATOES

The cold pack method of tomato preservation results in firm canned tomatoes, about two or three fruits in a small pint jar. Select healthy tomatoes that are uniformly red but still firm. Wash the jars, and heat them in boiling water, in a 200 degree F oven or in the dishwasher. Trim small decayed spots from the fruit. To remove the skins, heat them in boiling water for 30 to 60 seconds, and move them instantly into cool water before peeling. Wash jar sealer lids. Remove the tomato skins and cores and any green areas. Pack the tomatoes tightly, and cover with boiling water or boiling tomato juice. Carefully remove all air bubbles with a knife inserted down the inside edge of each jar, and add enough boiling water or juice to fill the jar to within 1 inch (for a quart or liter jar) or ½ inch (for a pint or half-liter jar) of the rim. To each small jar, add ½ tsp. salt and either

PICK OF THE CROP

Exposure of fruits to cool or chilling temperatures has a cumulative effect. The skin of tomato fruits progressively exposed to the cool nights of early fall gradually starts to break down. Hence, fruits harvested during this period do not keep well and are very susceptible to rotting. Mature green tomatoes are more sensitive to chilling injury than partly ripened fruits. Do not store mature green tomatoes in the refrigerator, since these tend to decay rapidly when later allowed to ripen at room temperature.

Pick tomatoes when fully ripe for best flavor, color and texture. Vine-ripened tomatoes store well for several weeks in the refrigerator. In the fall, harvest all ripe and mature green tomatoes before a predicted heavy frost. Mature green or turning tomatoes can be ripened satisfactorily indoors at temperatures between 60 degrees and 75 degrees F, although flavor of these tomatoes is not usually as good as that of vine-ripened fruits.

— **Growing Garden Tomatoes**

¼ tsp. citric acid or 1 Tbsp. reconstituted lemon juice. To medium (quart) jars, add 1 tsp. salt and either ½ tsp. citric acid or 2 Tbsp. lemon juice. Clean the rim of the jar with a clean, damp cloth. Apply sealer lid, and screw on band firmly. Process in a boiling water bath for 40 minutes for small jars and 50 minutes for medium jars, or process in a pressure canner at 5 pounds pressure for 10 minutes for pint and quart jars.

HOT PACK
STEWED TOMATOES

This method uses more tomatoes per jar than the cold pack method. Again, select healthy tomatoes that are uniformly red but still firm. Clean jars, and heat them in boiling water, in the oven at 200 degrees F or in the dishwasher. Wash tomatoes, and remove decayed spots. To remove the skins, heat them in boiling water for 30 to 60 seconds, and move them instantly into cool water before peeling. Wash jar sealer lids. Remove the tomato skins and cores and any green areas. Cut tomatoes in quarters, place in large pot, and heat gently, stirring frequently, to boiling. Pack hot in jars. Cover with boiling water or boiling tomato juice. Carefully remove all air bubbles with a knife inserted down the inside edge of each jar, and add enough boiling water or juice to fill the jar to within 1 inch (for a quart or liter jar) or ½ inch (for a pint or half-liter jar) of the rim. Add salt and lemon juice as noted for Whole Canned Tomatoes, clean rims, apply lids, and process pint jars in boiling water for 35 minutes, quarts for 45 minutes. Or process in a pressure canner at 5 pounds pressure for 8 minutes for pint and quart jars.

BASIC TOMATO SAUCE

This sauce can be used as a basis for spaghetti, lasagne, canneloni, manicotti or pizza, with or without the addition of ground beef and other vegetables.

¼ cup olive oil
1 clove garlic, minced
2 onions, diced
1 quart canned tomatoes
½ cup tomato paste
½ cup water
1½ tsp. salt
¼ tsp. pepper
1 tsp. basil
1 tsp. oregano
1 Tbsp. parsley
1 bay leaf
½ cup mushrooms, sliced

Heat olive oil in heavy saucepan. Add other ingredients in order listed. Simmer, uncovered, for 1 to 6 hours.
Add sliced mushrooms for the last 15 minutes.
— *Helen Shepherd*

TOMATO CATSUP

18 lbs. ripe tomatoes
2 cups chopped onions
1½ cups chopped sweet pepper
6 Tbsp. salt
4 cinnamon sticks
1 tsp. whole cloves
4 tsp. whole allspice
3 tsp. mustard seed
2 tsp. celery seed
2 cups sugar or substitute
3 cups vinegar

Wash tomatoes, core and cut into pieces. Combine with onions and peppers; cook 20 minutes. Press pulp through a fine sieve or a strainer. Tie spices in a cheesecloth bag, and add remaining ingredients. Boil until thickened. Remove spice bag; pour catsup into hot jars. Process 15 minutes.